Past Masters
General Editor   Keith Thomas

Muhammad

Michael Cook is a professor of Near Eastern studies at Princeton
University and the author of several books on the history of the
Middle East.

Postscript to 1996 reissue: Since 1977, the total number of Muslims has increased to just over a billion. They remain a little over a sixth of the world's population, while Christians amount to about a third. The number of Marxists, by contrast, is no longer significant, and probably never was; events since I wrote have fully borne out the scepticism expressed on this point by Mr Gulam Hyder of Peshawar in a letter he wrote to me in 1987.

Past Masters

Michael Cook

Muhammad

OXFORD
UNIVERSITY PRESS

OXFORD
UNIVERSITY PRESS

Great Clarendon Street, Oxford OX2 6DP

Oxford University Press is a department of the University of Oxford.
It furthers the University's objective of excellence in research, scholarship,
and education by publishing worldwide in

Oxford NewYork

Athens Auckland Bangkok Bogotá Buenos Aires Calcutta
Cape Town Chennai Dar es Salaam Delhi Florence Hong Kong Istanbul
Karachi Kuala Lumpur Madrid Melbourne Mexico City Mumbai
Nairobi Paris São Paulo Singapore Taipei Tokyo Toronto Warsaw

with associated companies in Berlin Ibadan

© Michael Cook 1983, 1996

First published 1983 as an Oxford University Press paperback
Reissued 1996

British Library Cataloguing in Publication Data

Data available

ISBN 0-19-287605-8

20 19 18 17 16 15 14

Printed in Great Britain by
Clays Ltd, St Ives plc

Preface

It is unlikely that Muhammad would have warmed to the series in which this book appears, or cared to be included in it. Its very title smacks of polytheism; the term 'master' is properly applicable only to God. He might also have resented the insinuation of intellectual originality. As a messenger of God, his task was to deliver a message, not to pursue his own fancies.

My own reservations about writing this book arise from different grounds. Muhammad made too great an impact on posterity for it to be an easy matter to place him in his original context. This is both a question of historical perspective and, as will appear, a question of sources. The result is that the only aspect of the book about which I feel no qualms is the brevity imposed by the format of the series. The attempt to write about Muhammad within such a compass has brought me to confront issues I might not otherwise have faced, and in ways which might not otherwise have occurred to me.

I give frequent references to the Koran (K), and occasional references to the *Sira* of Ibn Ishaq (S); for details, see below, p. 91. For simplicity I have transcribed Arabic names and terms without diacritics; note that the 's' and 'h' in the name 'Ibn Ishaq' are to be pronounced separately (more as in 'mishap' than in 'ship').

My thanks are due to Patricia Crone, Etan Kohlberg, Frank Stewart, Keith Thomas and Henry Hardy for their comments on a draft of this book; and to Fritz Zimmermann for a critical reading of what might otherwise have been the final version, and for a substantive influence on my understanding of Muslim theology.

Contents

Introduction

The Muslim world extends continuously from Senegal to Pakistan, and discontinuously eastwards to the Philippines. In 1977 there were some 720 million Muslims, just over a sixth of the world's population. The proportion might have been a great deal higher if the Muslims of Spain had applied themselves more energetically to the conquest of Europe in the eighth century, if the sudden death of Timur in 1405 had not averted a Muslim invasion of China, or if Muslims had played a more prominent role in the modern settlement of the New World and the Antipodes. But they have remained the major religious group in the heart of the Old World. In terms of sheer numbers they are outdone by the Christians, and arguably also by the Marxists. On the other hand, they are considerably less affected by sectarian divisions than either of these rivals: the overwhelming majority of Muslims belong to the Sunni mainstream of Islam.

There are many Muslims at the present day whose ancestors were infidels a thousand years ago; this is true by and large of the Turks, the Indonesians, and sizeable Muslim populations in India and Africa. The processes by which these peoples entered Islam were varied, and reflect a phase of Islamic history when different parts of the Muslim world had gone their separate ways. Yet the core of the Islamic community owes its existence to an earlier and more unitary historical context. Between the seventh and ninth centuries the Middle East and much of North Africa were ruled by the Caliphate, a Muslim state more or less coextensive with the Muslim world of its day. This empire in turn was the product of the

1

conquests undertaken by the inhabitants of the Arabian peninsula in the middle decades of the seventh century.

The men who effected these conquests were the followers of a certain Muhammad, an Arab merchant turned prophet and politician who in the 620s established a theocratic state among the tribes of western Arabia.

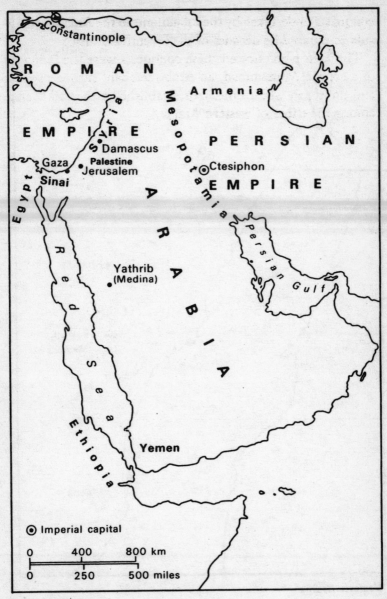

The Middle East

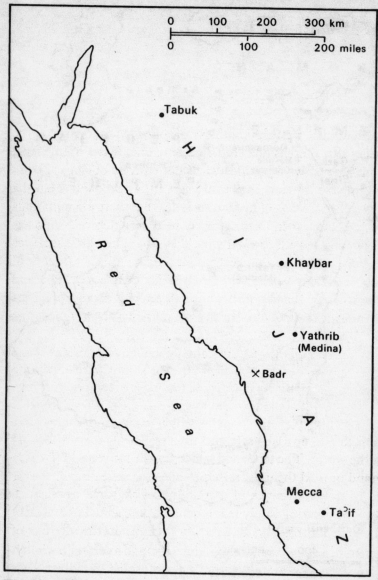

Western Arabia

1 Background

Muhammad was a monotheist prophet. Monotheism is the belief that there is one God, and only one. It is a simple idea; and like many simple ideas, it is not entirely obvious.

Over the last few thousand years it has probably been the general consensus of human societies that there are numerous gods (though men have certainly held very different views as to who these gods are and what they do). The oldest societies to have left us written records, and hence direct evidence of their religious beliefs, were polytheistic some five thousand years ago; by the first millennium BC there is enough evidence to indicate that polytheism was the religious norm right across the Old World.

It did not, however, remain unchallenged. In the same millennium ideas of a rather different stamp were appearing among the intellectual élites of the more advanced cultures. In Greece, Babylonia, India and China there emerged a variety of styles of thought which were noticeably more akin to our own abstract and impersonal manner of looking at the world. The tendency was to see the universe in terms of grand unified theories, rather than as the reflection of the ill-coordinated activities of a plurality of personal gods. Such ways of thinking rarely led to denial of the actual existence of the gods, but they tended to tidy them up in the interests of coherence and system, or to reduce them to a certain triviality. (Consider, for example, the view of some Buddhist sects that the gods are unable to attain enlightenment owing to the distracting behaviour of the goddesses.) What they

5

did not do was to pick out from the polytheistic heritage a single personal god, and discard the rest.

This development was to be the contribution of a conceptually less sophisticated people of the ancient Near East, the Israelites. Like other peoples of their world, the Israelites possessed a national god who was closely identified with their political and military fortunes. Like others, they experienced the desolation of defeat and exile at the hands of more powerful enemies. Their distinctive reaction to this history was to develop an *exclusive* cult of their national god, eventually proclaimed as the only god in existence – in a word, as God.

Had monotheism remained a peculiarity of the Israelites (or as we can now call them, the Jews), it would not have ranked as more than a curiosity in the history of the world at large. As it happened, this situation was drastically changed by a minor Jewish heresy which became a world religion: Christianity. Its primary spread was within the Roman Empire. By the fourth century after Christ it had been adopted as the state religion; by the sixth century the Roman Empire was more or less solidly Christian. At the same time Christianity had spread unevenly in several directions beyond the imperial frontiers. There were, for example, Christian kingdoms in Armenia and Ethiopia; and although the Persian Empire held fast to its ancestral Zoroastrian faith, it contained within its borders a significant Christian minority, particularly in Mesopotamia. West of India, no major society was unshaken by the rise of monotheism, and only the Persians stood out against it.

Arabia

South of the Roman and Persian Empires lay the world's largest desert. This area is divided into two unequal portions by the Red Sea: to the west lies the Sahara, and to the east Arabia. The Arabian peninsula is a vast rectangle, some 1,300 miles long and 750 wide, stretching south-east from the Fertile Crescent (i.e. Syria and Mesopotamia). Its predominant feature is its aridity. This is slightly offset in the north, where desert gives way to semi-desert and even to steppe, and still more in the south, where a mountainous terrain receives a measure of summer rain. But between these marginal zones lies the bulk of Arabia, and for the most part it is desert relieved only by scattered oases.

In comparison with the Fertile Crescent, Arabia was accordingly a land of deprivation. Agriculture, the basic economic activity of mankind between the neolithic and industrial revolutions, was largely confined to the oases; and even the rainfall agriculture of the Yemen was derisory by comparison with what could be achieved across the Red Sea in Ethiopia. Much of Arabia was fit only for pastoralism, and a nomadic pastoralism at that.

These conditions did much to shape the character of Arabian society. Civilisation, with its cities, temples, bureaucracies, aristocracies, priesthoods, regular armies, and elaborate cultural heritages, requires a substantial agricultural base. With the partial exception of the Yemen, such an edifice could not be built in Arabia. Arabian society was tribal, in the oases as much as in the desert. There were pariah groups excluded from tribal society, and 'kings' who were almost but not quite above it; but by the standards of the Fertile Crescent, Arabian society was egalitarian and anarchic. By the same standards the culture of Arabia was simple, if not threadbare; its principal legacy is its poetry.

The isolating peninsular geography of Arabia, and the mobility of pastoralists within it, contributed to another significant feature of Arabian society, its homogeneity. To a surprising extent, the Arabian desert was the land of a single people, the Arabs, speaking a single language, Arabic. This cannot always have been so. The Arabs do not appear by name before the ninth century BC, and were not the first nomadic pastoralists of the area; but by the time of Muhammad, any earlier diversity had been obliterated north of the Yemen.

Although Arabian society was very different from the settled societies of the Fertile Crescent and beyond, it was by no means deprived of contact with the outside world. Yet these contacts, though ancient, had wrought no transformation on either side; their effects were most pronounced in the border areas where the two patterns interacted.

We may begin by looking at the military and political aspect of this relationship. A nomadic tribal society is warlike and highly mobile; but it is also allergic to large-scale organisation. As raiders, the tribesmen of Arabia were accordingly a persistent nuisance to the settled world; but they were rarely a serious military threat. The Nabatean Arabs built up a kingdom on the edge of the desert which in 85 BC occupied Damascus, and an Arab queen of the later fourth century invaded Palestine; but such events were exceptional. They might lead to the creation of Arab statelets, and encourage penetration by Arab settlers, but they initiated no massive and enduring conquests. A state governing a settled society, by contrast, is capable of organised military effort on a large scale, and may adopt a more or less forward policy of frontier defence against nomadic raiders. It has, however, neither the means nor the motive for conquering a desert. An eccentric Babylonian king had once spent several years in the western Arabian oases, and a Roman expedition had blundered through the Arabian desert on its way to the Yemen; but again such episodes were exceptional. Under normal conditions, the political influence of outside powers was confined to frontier areas, where it might lead to the formation of Arab client principalities and the use of their troops as auxiliaries. It is true that a certain departure from this pattern seems to have arisen from the imperial rivalries of the centuries preceding the career of Muhammad. In this period the Persians established a hegemony over the Arabs on an unprecedented scale. They were entrenched in the east and south, and even had some presence in the oases of central Arabia. But it is hard to imagine this yoke as a heavy one in inner Arabia, least of all in the west, and it scarcely appears in the story of Muhammad's life.

Another significant form of contact with the outside world was trade. The Islamic sources remember a trade in silver to Persia from south and central Arabia, in close connection with the Persian political hegemony. In the west they describe an Arab trade with southern Syria of which the staple commodity would seem to have been leather. By the standards of the international trade of the day, both the silver and, still more, the leather trades were doubtless rather trivial. Frankincense, the great Arabian export of antiquity, had long ago lost its market in the Roman Empire; and coffee, the only other Arabian export of consequence before the arrival of oil, had not yet appeared. At the same time the bulk of the peninsula played no part in international transit trade; it was naturally cheaper to ship goods round the peninsula than to transport them across it. But such trade as there was sufficed to ensure that a knowledge of the civilised world and its proceedings existed far into Arabia.

Arabia and monotheism

The Arabs were polytheists. The pattern of their religion was simple – the Arabs did not, for example, provide their gods with expensive housing such as was standard in the Fertile Crescent, and so far as we know they developed little in the way of a religious mythology. But simple as it was, such

9

indications as we have suggest that it had been remarkably stable over a long period; thus Allat, a goddess prominent in the time of Muhammad, is already attested by Herodotus in the fifth century BC. In the centuries preceding the life of Muhammad, however, external influences were beginning to disturb this ancient polytheism. Predominantly, this influence was monotheist; despite the Persian hegemony, the impact of Zoroastrianism seems to have been slight outside the north-east.

As might be expected, the Arabs were affected by the rise of Christianity, and more particularly by the sects which came to predominate among their settled neighbours. In Syria, the prevailing doctrine from the fifth century was that of the Monophysites; this sect achieved a considerable following among the Arab tribes of the northern desert. In the Persian Empire the Christian population was mainly Nestorian, and to a lesser extent this sect held an analogous position among the neighbouring Arabs. It was also active along the Arab side of what in political terms was very much the Persian Gulf. In the Yemen we hear most of Monophysites, matching as it happened the form of Christianity which prevailed in Ethiopia.

There was also a considerable, and probably much older, Jewish presence in western Arabia. The Islamic tradition describes substantial Jewish populations in several of the western oases, in the region known as the Hijaz, and this has some confirmation from archaeology. In the Yemen a Jewish presence is likewise attested. There is evidence that it was in contact with the Jews of Palestine, and it seems to have achieved some local influence; in the early sixth century a Yemeni king martyred Christians in the name of Judaism.

Despite this Christian and Jewish penetration, Arabian society was still predominantly pagan; but an awareness of monotheism in one or other of its forms must have been widespread.

If we imagine ourselves for a moment in sixth-century Arabia, what long-term expectations could we reasonably have entertained? First, that if the Arabs had never in the past been a serious military threat to the outside world, they were unlikely to become one now. Second, that the escalating rivalry between the leading foreign powers, the Romans and the Persians, would lead if anything to a tightening of their grip on whatever was worth controlling in Arabia. And third, that despite the persistence of paganism and the presence of Judaism, it was only a matter of time before Arabia became more or less Christian. In the event, the triumph of monotheism in Arabia took a form which rendered each of these plausible expectations false.

2 Life

The life of Muhammad is the subject of a wealth of Muslim narrative sources. Of these the most successful in the Muslim world, and the best-known outside it, is a life of the Prophet composed about the middle of the eighth century by a certain Ibn Ishaq. We possess it in the edition of a minor scholar two generations his junior. Much, though not all, of what is said in this chapter derives from this work. My aim here is simply to present the traditional account in outline – not, at this point, to interpret it or assess its reliability.

Mecca

Muhammad was born into the Arab tribe of Quraysh in the southern Hijaz. Quraysh are defined as the descendants in the male line of a certain Fihr ibn Malik, who lived eleven generations before Muhammad. They were a noble lineage, but not at first a particularly successful one. For several generations they lived scattered among a wider tribal grouping, and did not function as a political unit. Nor did they possess a territorial centre; Mecca, a local sanctuary of great antiquity, was in other hands. Five generations before Muhammad, this situation was remedied by an enterprising member of the tribe called Qusayy. He put together an alliance, and by war and diplomacy obtained possession of the Meccan sanctuary. He was then able to ingather his scattered fellow-tribesmen and to settle them in Mecca. They held him in such respect that he was virtually their king – a position which was not enjoyed by any of his descendants. Thus was established the society into which Muhammad was born.

But how, one might ask, did the newly settled Quraysh make ends meet? Mecca is situated in a notoriously barren valley, which as such is quite unsuited to supporting a settled population. The answer appears in the third generation before Muhammad, when Hashim, grandson of Qusayy and great-grandfather of the Prophet, took steps to establish Quraysh as merchants of international standing. He initiated the two caravan journeys of the year, one in the summer and one in the winter. He made a friend of the Roman Emperor and obtained protection for merchants of Quraysh in Roman territory; he himself died in the Palestinian town of Gaza. His brothers obtained similar concessions from the rulers of Persia, the Yemen and Ethiopia, and at the same time arrangements were made to secure the safety of Meccan trade in the territories of the intervening Arab tribes. In this way was created the mercantile economy in which Muhammad himself was in due course to play a part.

Despite these developments, Quraysh remained very much a part of the local scene. Socially and culturally, they were well integrated into the world of the neighbouring pastoralists, with whom their relations were close and on balance friendly. Mecca itself was a city only in name. In the generation before Muhammad, most of its dwellings were still mere huts constructed of palm-branches; dramatic redevelopment overtook the town only in the very different conditions of the early Islamic period.

Mecca also remained a sanctuary, and so a centre of pilgrimage. In the eyes of the tradition, as we shall see, it had originally been a monotheist foundation, but by the period which concerns us it was effectively a pagan sanctuary. Qusayy, at the time of his take-over, had left the rites of pilgrimage unchanged, but had made practical arrangements for the feeding of the pilgrims. This responsibility was in due course inherited by the Prophet's grandfather, who also rediscovered and restored the spring originally associated with the sanctuary. In Muhammad's youth the central shrine of the sanctuary, the building known as the Ka'ba, was reconstructed; Muhammad himself participated at a crucial juncture. There were also stirrings of monotheism in the generation before Muhammad, with three of the four men affected ending up as Christians; but Mecca remained an over-whelmingly pagan society.

Early life

Muhammad was born at an uncertain date around AD 570. (At his death in 632, he was aged sixty, sixty-three or sixty-five according to one's choice of authorities.) He did not receive his mission as a prophet till the age of forty (or forty-three or forty-five), i.e. around the year 610.

Prior to this there was, as might be expected, no lack of pointers to his future greatness. At his birth there issued with him a light by which his mother could see the castles of Bostra in Syria. Prophecies regarding his future role came from Arab soothsayers, from Jews, and from Christians of various kinds. On one occasion he accompanied his uncle Abu Talib on a caravan journey to Syria; a Christian monk recognised the boy for what he was, and advised his uncle to take great care to protect him from the Jews.

Yet at a more mundane level his prospects during much of this period were anything but assured. His father died before, or not long after, he was born. Soon after birth he was handed over to foster-parents in an impoverished neighbouring tribe for two or three years; he then returned to his mother, who herself died when he was six. After being cared for by his grandfather for a couple of years, he went to live with the family of Abu Talib, and this uncle became in effect a father to him. Then as a young man he was retained by Khadija, a wealthy widow, to act as her commercial agent in the trade with Syria; he did well, and in due course she saw fit to marry him. He was thus, at this stage, a somewhat marginal figure, who owed such success as he had achieved as much to his older and richer wife as to his own position in society.

Mission

Eventually Muhammad was given his prophetic mission. He had been in the habit of spending one month of each year on the nearby Mount Hira'. This, it would seem, was a religious custom of pagan times; while there, he might be joined by his family, and would feed such of the poor as came to him. One night while he was residing on the mountain in this fashion the angel Gabriel visited him in his sleep, and ordered him to recite; in response to Muhammad's puzzlement he then taught him a passage of the 96th chapter of the Koran, which appropriately begins with the command 'recite!'. The experience was in two ways characteristic of what followed: Gabriel was to be the normal channel of communication between God and Muhammad, and it was in such fragments that what was to become the Muslim scripture, the Koran, was gradually revealed to him. At the time, however, Muhammad found the experience disturbing, and concluded that he must be either a poet or possessed – in either case the victim of a malign spirit. But a local Christian perceived that Muhammad's experience was comparable to that of Moses, and inferred him to be 'the prophet of this people'; while a careful experiment devised by Muhammad's wife Khadija established that his supernatural visitor was indeed an angel and not a devil.

After receiving his mission, Muhammad spent fifteen (or thirteen, or ten) years in Mecca. During this period the episodic revelation of scripture continued, and a simple ritual and morality were developed. The ritual consisted of a number (fixed at five) of daily prayers, to be performed in a state of ritual purity attained by washing; the practical details were demonstrated to Muhammad by Gabriel. The morality comprised such principles as abstaining from theft and fornication. This was also the time when Muhammad was vouchsafed a remarkable supernatural journey. One night while he was sleeping in the sanctuary in Mecca, he was taken by Gabriel to Jerusalem; there he met Abraham, Moses and Jesus, and led them in prayer, after which he was taken on a visit to heaven. His subsequent description of the layout of Jerusalem was confirmed, presumably from personal experience, by one of his followers. At the same time, the authenticity of his mission continued to be confirmed by a variety of Christians, not least of whom was the ruler of Ethiopia.

In the course of this period Muhammad made a considerable number of Meccan converts. At first (if we follow Ibn Ishaq) these converts were confined to his immediate family: Khadija, his wife; 'Ali, a young son of Abu Talib whom Muhammad had taken into his household at the time of a famine; and Zayd, a slave whom he had manumitted. For three years the incipient religion continued to be a private matter. Then God ordered Muhammad to make it public, and it rapidly acquired a local following, and became the talk of Arabia.

The reaction of the pagan Meccans to this development was initially a tolerant one. There was no reason, as one of them put it, why a man should not choose a religion for himself as he pleased. There was some mockery and cynicism – suggestions that Muhammad had actually received his supposedly divine message from human sources – but there was no real trouble until Muhammad began to disparage the local pagan gods. This was considered offensive. Even then, the pagans showed great willingness to compromise; they offered to make Muhammad a king, or to obtain suitable medical treatment for his psychic condition. Certainly on the one occasion when Muhammad temporarily yielded to the temptation to allow the pagan gods a place in his religion, the move was in human terms a dramatic success. But it was not monotheism. Muhammad reverted to the purity of his message, and relations between his followers and their pagan fellow-tribesmen became bitterly hostile.

What follows is crucial for Muhammad's career, and must be seen against the background of tribal politics in a stateless society. Since the days of its founder Qusayy, the Meccan polity had lacked a central authority; it was made up of a number of descent groups whose mutual relations could easily degenerate into civil war. To some extent, the spread of the new religion reflected these divisions: it was strongest among the Banu Hashim, the descendants of Hashim, to whom Muhammad himself belonged; and it was weakest among their leading rivals, the Banu 'Abd Shams. This situation lay behind the boycott which the pagans for some two or three years imposed on the Banu Hashim and their nearest relatives, refusing intermarriage or commercial dealings with them until such time as they came to their senses in the matter of Muhammad. But alignments were not in fact as clearcut as this suggests. Leading members of the Banu Hashim remained pagans, while at the same time a good many members of other descent groups converted to Muhammad's religion.

The question for the Muslims was who, in this stateless society, would protect them. The most exposed were clearly those outside the Prophet's own descent group. They were wide open to attack by members of their own descent groups, and there was nothing in the circumstances which

17

Muhammad could do to protect them. It was in response to this situation that Muhammad sent a party of his followers to take refuge in Ethiopia, where they succeeded in obtaining the protection of the ruler. For a long time Muhammad's own position was relatively secure; thanks to the strong personal commitment of his pagan uncle Abu Talib, he enjoyed the protection of his own descent group. But in due course Abu Talib died, and Muhammad's problem now became acute.

His only recourse was to look outside Mecca for the protection he needed – an expedient already foreshadowed in the Ethiopian episode. But the Ethiopian ruler was obviously too distant to provide protection in Arabia itself, and Muhammad began his search nearer home. A visit to the neighbouring town of Ta'if proved a fiasco; its only happy moment was the recognition of Muhammad's prophethood by a Christian slave from Nineveh. Thereafter Muhammad presented himself at fairs as a prophet in search of protectors, and made overtures to a number of tribes; but he was always turned down. Finally deliverance came from the north.

The hijra

Medina, or Yathrib to use its pre-Islamic name, was a very different sort of place from Mecca. It was one of a number of agriculturally rich oases in the Hijaz. Like others of these oases, it had an ancient Jewish population. These Jews were tribesmen well assimilated to the Arabian environment. At a later date Arabs had settled alongside the Jews; they constituted the tribes of Aws and Khazraj, and had come to dominate the oasis. Like Mecca, Yathrib lacked a central authority. Unlike Mecca, it was disturbed by recurrent civil strife. It was these features of the oasis that were to give Muhammad his opening.

On one occasion when he was advertising his cause at a fair,

Muhammad had the good fortune to identify a small group of Khazraj. He invited these six men to sit down with him, and proceeded to expound his religion. The group responded positively for two reasons. Their close relations with the Jews of their city had familiarised them with the notion that a new prophet was about to appear; and they saw Muhammad's cause as one in which the people of Yathrib might be united, a solution to their domestic political problems. 'If God unites them in it', they added to Muhammad, 'no man will be more powerful than you' (S 198).

It was some time before anything came of this project; but eventually Muhammad reached a firm agreement with a larger and more representative group of tribesmen from Yathrib. The tribesmen pledged themselves to protect him as they would their own families, and showed themselves willing to accept the risks which that entailed – in particular the likelihood of military confrontation with Quraysh. Muhammad then ordered his Meccan followers to leave the city and emigrate to Yathrib. He himself stayed behind until such time as he received God's permission to emigrate; when this came, he fled his native city and joined his followers.

Muhammad's 'emigration' from Mecca to Yathrib took place in the Christian year 622, and is called the *hijra*; the year in which it fell was later adopted as the first of the Muslim era. Those of Muhammad's Meccan followers who made the journey were known as the 'emigrants' (*muhajirun*). His local followers in Yathrib, by contrast, were his 'helpers' (*ansar*). All alike were 'believers' or 'Muslims'; the literal sense of the latter is perhaps 'those who submit', i.e. to God, and it is from such 'submission' (*islam*) that Muhammad's religion takes its name. From the time of the *hijra* onwards, we can speak of Yathrib as the 'city' of the Prophet, Medina. Excursions apart, he remained there for a decade, from the *hijra* in 622 to his death in 632.

The umma

One of Muhammad's first tasks in Medina was to create a political order – one which would give him and his followers the protection they needed, and rid Medina of its domestic strife. The arrangements which Muhammad made are embodied in a document which has come to be known as the 'Constitution of Medina'. This document declares the existence of a community or people (*umma*) made up of Muhammad's followers, both those of Quraysh and those of Yathrib. To this community belong also the Jews, subject to the qualification that they follow their own religion. Just as important, the document establishes an authority within the community: any serious dispute between the parties to the document must be referred to God and Muhammad. From the mass of stipulations making up the rest of the document, two themes are worth picking out. One is a concern to clarify the relationship between the new community and the existing tribal structure; this is particularly apparent in the regulations regarding the payment of bloodwit and the ransoming of captives. The other is the fact that a major interest of the parties of the document is the waging of war. There are stipulations regarding the initiation and termination of hostilities, contribution to their cost, and so forth. Jews contribute, and fight alongside the believers.

As might be expected, the consolidation of this community did not proceed without tension or conflict. The most violent episodes concerned Muhammad's relations with the Medinese Jewish tribes. Against a background of Jewish jealousy at the fact that God had chosen His latest prophet from among the Arabs, relations broke down with one Jewish tribe after another. In the second year of the *hijra*, a trivial quarrel precipitated hostilities with the Banu Qaynuqa', who were then expelled from Medina. In the fourth year they were followed into exile by the Banu 'l-Nadir, who had plotted to assassinate Muhammad.

In the fifth the Banu Qurayza sided with Muhammad's external enemies who were besieging him in Medina; the outcome was the mass execution of the men and the enslavement of the women and children. Thereafter the Jews played no part in Muhammad's polity, though a few remained as converts.

There were also tensions among Muhammad's Arab followers. The Medinese *ansar* had an abiding suspicion of the Meccan *muhajirun* and their kinship with Muhammad; they readily flared up at the suggestion that the Meccans were taking over. And although overt paganism rapidly disappeared in Medina, there remained a group whose outward acceptance of Muhammad's religion covered an inner scepticism and disaffection. The leading representative of these 'hypocrites' (*munafiqun*) was 'Abdallah ibn Ubayy, an ambitious tribesman who had almost succeeded in establishing himself as king in Medina when Muhammad arrived. His temporising was responsible for the fact that the Banu Qaynuqa' were expelled rather than killed; he left Muhammad in the lurch just before the major military disaster of his career; and he played a part in articulating the resentment of the *ansar* against the *muhajirun*. At no point, however, did such tensions degenerate into civil war.

War

The most prominent feature of Muhammad's years in Medina was warfare against external enemies. The 'Constitution of Medina' presupposes that there is a war on, and the sources list dozens of military enterprises, ranging from major expeditions led by Muhammad himself, to commando raids to assassinate individual enemies of the Prophet.

The central theme in this activity was Muhammad's confrontation with his home town of Mecca. In the second year of the *hijra* he made plans to intercept a rich Meccan caravan returning from Syria. The caravan escaped, but a force sent out by the Meccans to defend it was roundly defeated by some three hundred Muslims (reinforced by angels) at Badr. Subsequently, however, it looked as if Muhammad had taken on more than he could handle. The next two rounds were fought in the immediate neighbourhood of Medina: in the third year Muhammad suffered his major defeat at Uhud; and in the fifth he was defending Medina itself. In the following year, however, we find him attempting a peaceful pilgrimage to Mecca; the Meccans prevented him, but a truce was negotiated between the two parties. Thereafter the tide turned, leading in the eighth year to the surrender of Mecca and Muhammad's triumphant entry into the city which had rejected him.

As his fortunes improved, Muhammad achieved military successes in other directions as well. In the seventh year he had taken possession of two major Jewish oases of the Hijaz, Khaybar and Fadak. The conquest of Mecca led on to a consolidation of his power in the southern Hijaz: an alliance of hostile tribes was defeated nearby at Hunayn, and the oasis of Ta'if submitted. In the aftermath of these successes, the Arab tribes at large more or less voluntarily submitted to Muhammad's authority.

One theatre of Muhammad's military activities had a particular significance for the future. In the far north-west, tribal Arabia bordered on the Roman Empire. Early in the eighth year of the *hijra*, before the conquest of Mecca, Muhammad had sent an expedition to this region without success. In the following year he himself went as far as Tabuk, but without confronting the Romans. In the eleventh year he planned to send an expedition into Roman territory in Palestine, but his death intervened. Within a generation of his death these small beginnings had issued in the Muslim conquest of the Middle East.

The faith

Muhammad's years in Medina were also important in more narrowly religious terms. They saw a spread of his religion closely associated with his military success. Among the pagan Arabs, resistance to his message – as opposed to his political authority – was rarely deep-rooted, though the attachment of the people of Ta'if to their pagan idols was something of an exception. The Jews and Christians of Arabia (particularly the former) proved more stiff-necked – whence Muhammad's prescription on his death-bed to the effect that they be expelled from Arabia. Outside Arabia, Muhammad addressed himself to the rulers of the day with varying results. The king of Ethiopia whole-heartedly accepted Muhammad's message; the Roman Emperor privately conceded its truth; the ruler of Persia tore up the letter he was sent. Meanwhile lesser imitators of Muhammad had appeared in eastern and southern Arabia, a backhanded compliment to the success of his mission.

At the same time Muhammad's religion was itself elaborated and perfected. He continued to receive revelations, and by the time of his death the entire content of the Koran had been revealed. The basic rituals and duties of Islam were established or further refined: washing, prayer, alms-giving, fasting, pilgrimage. Numerous prescriptions on matters of religious law were revealed to Muhammad as part of the Koran, or otherwise stipulated by him. On the occasion of the conquest of Khaybar, for example, he declared the eating of the flesh of the domesticated ass forbidden.

A particularly dramatic moment in the development of the religion was the changing of the direction in which the believers prayed. This took place in the second year of the *hijra*. Previously they had faced Jerusalem in prayer, like the Jews; from now on they faced towards their own sanctuary of Mecca. This

reorientation was eventually complemented by Muslim possession of the sanctuary itself. At the time of the conquest of Mecca
in the eighth year, Muhammad purged the sanctuary of its
pagan idols; and in the tenth year he demonstrated in detail the
Muslim rites of pilgrimage.

In the eleventh year of the *hijra* (AD 632) Muhammad was taken
ill in Medina and died. He left behind him nine widows and an
Egyptian concubine. By the latter he had had a son, Abraham,
who died in infancy; of his other children, four daughters
survived him.

3 The monotheist universe

In the following four chapters I shall set out the fundamental
ideas associated with Muhammad's mission. I shall draw pri-
marily on the Koran, which we have already met as the corpus
of the revelations received by Muhammad through Gabriel at
sundry times. I shall also make use of the abundant traditions
which relate what Muhammad said and did, and are preserved
in Ibn Ishaq's biography and other such sources; occasionally I
shall fill out the picture with views ascribed to early Muslims
but not directly attributed to Muhammad. Any substantial
use of these non-Koranic materials will be indicated. How far
the resulting picture can be considered to represent the actual
teaching of Muhammad is a question to be taken up in a later
chapter.

The universe in a nutshell

There are two components of Muhammad's universe: God
and the world. Of these, God is the more remarkable. He is
eternal – He has always existed, and always will. He is omni-
scient: not a leaf falls without His knowledge. He is omnipotent: when He decides something, He has only to say 'Be!'
and it is. Above all, He is unique: He is one, and there is no
other god but Him; He has no partners in His divinity. Fur-
thermore, He is merciful and beneficent – but for reasons we
shall come to, He is frequently angry.

The rest of the universe – the seven heavens, the earths,
and their contents – was created by Him and belongs to Him.
This feat of creation was achieved in six days (though the
days in question would seem to have been divine days, each

equivalent to a thousand human years). The basic structure of the world is fairly simple, although the scanty Koranic data have to be completed from tradition. The lower part, which was created first, consisted originally of a single earth which God then split into seven. The seven earths are arranged one above another like a stack of plates; we inhabit the top one, and the devil the bottom one, which is hell. Above the earths God placed an analogous stack of heavens; the lowest heaven is our own sky, the topmost is Paradise. The scale is generous by terrestrial standards: the standard distance, that between any two neighbouring plates, takes five hundred years to traverse, and larger dimensions are encountered at the top and bottom. The whole structure is said to have posed serious underpinning problems, to which colourful solutions were found; but these and other details need not detain us. God, in so far as He may be said to be in any particular place, is at the top of the world. Having created it, He did not leave it to run itself, or delegate the responsibility to others. Rather He continues to attend to it in every detail. He holds back the sky to prevent it falling on the earth; and He it is who makes rain to fall and trees to grow.

The world contains more than one form of intelligent life; but it is mankind which receives the lion's share of divine attention. The human race is monogenetic: we all descend from Adam, who was made from dust, and his consort, who was fashioned from him. We too belong to God. Tradition, slightly adapting a Koranic passage, relates that after creating Adam God rubbed his back, and there issued from him the souls of all future humanity. God then called them to bear witness, asking: 'Am I not your Lord?', to which they replied 'Yes, we bear witness' (K 7.171).

Despite this admission, the record of human conduct has to a large extent been one of disobedience to God. In the varied repertoire of human disobedience, one sin is particularly prominent: the failure to accord to Him the exclusive worship which is His due. This sin of polytheism is one into which men keep falling, and which then acquires for them the spurious authority of ancestral tradition. Hence the repeated dispatch of divine messengers to prise men loose from the ways of their fathers and revive their primordial allegiance to God alone. The story of these reminders, and the mixed reception they met with, makes up the core of human history; we shall take it up in the following chapter.

Sooner rather than later, this history will end in a cataclysmic destruction of the world as we know it. The sky will be split, the stars scattered, the earth pounded to dust. The entire human race will be brought back to life – an easy matter for God to bring about, as the Koran insists. He will then proceed to judge men according to their deeds with the aid of balances; the saved will spend the rest of eternity amid the colourful delights of Paradise, while those found wanting are consigned to the pains of hell.

The universe in comparative perspective

In these basic outlines, Muhammad's universe does not differ radically from those of other monotheist faiths. What comment it requires will accordingly depend on whether the reader is himself from a monotheist background. If he is, it will be enough to identify the more significant points of comparison. If he is not, he may legitimately find the entire conception puzzling; and this is perhaps where we should begin.

Historically, monotheism is descended from the polytheism of the ancient Near East. Near Eastern gods were often human beings writ large: they had bodies of human shape, quarrelled, behaved irresponsibly when drunk, and so forth. The God of the Old Testament was not given to such undignified behaviour, but He retained considerable traces from this past. The Bible speaks of Him as creating man in His own image, and as taking a day's rest after the labour of creation; and it treats in detail of the manner in which the Deity is to be housed and supplied with food. The tendency in monotheism has, however, been away from such a human conception of God, and towards a more transcendent one. Muhammad's God in some respects illustrates this trend. Admittedly the Koran still speaks freely of God's 'hand', and refers to Him settling into His throne; but it strongly denies that He found the work of creation tiring, and Islam does not accept the notion that God created man in His own image.

This dehumanisation of God had one rather serious implication, and we can best identify it by going back to the Mesopotamian myth which explains the creation of man. Even after the basic work of creation had been done, it must be understood, the running of the universe made heavy demands on the gods; and as might be expected, it was the junior gods who were saddled with the drudgery. Under these conditions, serious labour unrest developed among the junior gods, and a critical situation was defused only when discussions among their seniors issued in the creation of a substitute race, namely mankind. Since then men have done the hard work, and by and large the gods have lived a life of leisure. The whole story turns on the assumption that the gods have needs close enough to our own to be immediately intelligible to us, and that their powers to satisfy these needs, though considerable, are not unlimited.

The monotheist God, by contrast, needs nothing and nobody: 'God has no need of the worlds' (K 3.92), and 'no need of you' (K 39.9); and if He were to need anything, He has only to say 'Be!' and it is. What then can be the point of His having human servants, or indeed a created world at all? Yet the

Koran often refers to such servants of God, and explicitly assures us that God did not create heaven and earth for fun; had He wished to amuse Himself, He could have done so without resorting to the creation of an external world. But by the same token, the world cannot be considered to meet any other divine need. The strong and often immediate sense of God's purposes that characterises monotheism thus fits badly with the sublimer notions it has developed about His nature.

The reader who is himself from a monotheist background will of course be inured to this tension. He should also find the basic conception of Muhammad's universe a familiar one; it is not so distant from that found in the first chapter of the Book of Genesis, and ultimately derives from it. Other features have parallels in monotheist cosmology as it existed closer to the time of Muhammad. Thus the seven heavens, the five-hundred-year module, and the underpinning arrangements can all be matched from Jewish tradition. Similarly homespun ideas were also current among the Christians of the Middle East; here, however, they were under strong pressure from the very different style of cosmological thought represented by Greek philosophy. A sixth-century Nestorian Christian found it necessary to write at length to defend his traditional monotheist image of God's world against this pernicious influence. The same influence was later at work in the Islamic world, but not in the period which concerns us.

The feature of Muhammad's universe which is most likely to strike a non-Muslim monotheist as alien is a certain bleakness in the relationship between God's power and human action. This point is intimately related to the general tension within monotheism that we have already explored: on the one hand God frequently engages in behaviour that can be understood in much the same way as our own (e.g. He keeps sending messengers to disobedient communities with warnings they mostly disregard); and on the other hand, He is an omnipotent God who can realise His wishes immediately (e.g. He could if He wished have all men believe in Him). The first conception suggests that men act of their own free will, and sooner or later get their deserts for it. The second suggests that human acts, like other events, take place because God in His omnipotence has decreed that they will. The two conceptions do not go well together, if indeed they are compatible at all.

In the circumstances, there are two obvious ways to respond to the dilemma. One is to cut back the operation of God's omnipotence to allow at least a minimal domain for the freedom of human choice; for if men are not given enough moral rope to hang themselves, we are confronted with the unwelcome implication that their sin and damnation are the fault of God. This, essentially, was the option chosen by the other monotheist faiths of the day. The second course is to stand unflinchingly by God's omnipotence, and to allow human free will to be swamped by it; this, essentially, is the direction in which Islam inclines. God 'leads astray whom He will and guides whom He will' (K 16.95). He has created many men for hell, and pledged His word to fill it. The unbelievers will not believe, whether Muhammad warns them or not, for 'God has set a seal on their hearts' (K 2.6). This idiom was not new in monotheism; the God of Exodus repeatedly hardened the heart of Pharaoh the better to display His signs (see for example Exod. 7.3, and compare Rom. 9.17–18). Nor is it one consistently used in the Koran. Thus Muhammad is told to say: 'The truth is from your Lord; so let whosoever will, believe, and let whosoever will, disbelieve' (K 18.28). Such verses were duly cited by the proponents of the doctrine of human free will in Islam. But for better or worse, they fought a losing battle.

4 Monotheist history

Early Muslim scholars assigned to this world a duration of some six or seven thousand years. By the standards of ancient Indian or modern Western cosmology such a figure is breathtakingly small, but it agreed well enough with the views of other monotheists. Of this span, it was clear that the greater part had already elapsed – perhaps 5,500 out of 6,000 years. Muhammad's mission thus fell decidedly late in the day. He himself is said to have told his followers, with reference to the prospective duration of their community: 'Your appointed time compared with that of those who were before you is as from the afternoon prayer to the setting of the sun.' The formulation is problematic, but there is learned authority for the view that it represents about one-fourteenth of the total.

An early scholar who reckoned the age of the world at 5,600 years avowed that he knew about every period of its history, and what kings and prophets had lived in it. We can disregard the kings; it is the prophets who constitute the backbone of monotheist history. The list given below shows the most important of them. (The dates, which may be taken to represent years elapsed since the expulsion of Adam from Paradise, have the authority of Ibn Ishaq; but conflicting opinions abound on such details.)

Adam	–
Noah	1200
Abraham	2342
Moses	2907
Jesus	4832
Muhammad	5432

A chronology of this kind is not to be found in the Koran; but all the prophets listed here appear there, and their order in time is clearly envisaged as shown.

Adam to Jesus

Every name in the list bar the last is familiar from the Bible. The first four names are major figures of the Pentateuch, and as such the common property of Judaism and Christianity. The parts they play in the Koranic view of monotheist history are more or less in accordance with their Biblical roles – though a good deal of material is altered, added or lost. Adam remains the common ancestor of humanity, and is expelled from Paradise with his consort for eating forbidden fruit. Noah is the builder of the ark whose occupants alone survive the flood in which God destroys the human race. Abraham is still the father who nearly sacrifices his son to God. Moses confronts Pharaoh, leads the Israelite exodus from Egypt, and meets God on Mount Sinai; to him is revealed a scripture, the Pentateuch. Other Old Testament figures also appear, notably Joseph, David and Solomon.

All this is familiar. Yet there are differences, and of these the most significant is a subtle shift of emphasis. The original Biblical figures play roles of considerable diversity; the Koran, by contrast, has a tendency to impose on them a stereotyped conception of the monotheist messenger. Thus in the Koran, Noah's mission is to warn his polytheist contemporaries to worship God alone; whereas in the Bible their sin is moral corruption rather than polytheism, and Noah has in any case no message to deliver to them.

With the next name on the list we come to a specifically Christian figure. As might be expected, the Jesus of the Koran is still recognisable as the Jesus of the New Testament: he is styled the Messiah, is born of a virgin, works miracles, has disciples, is rejected by the Jews, and eventually ascends to heaven. There are, however, divergences. For no obvious reason the Koran insists that Jesus was not really crucified; and there is no sense of his mission being addressed to an audience wider than the Children of Israel. But the crucial point of divergence is the insistence that Jesus, though a messenger of God, was not His son, still less God Himself. He is accordingly quoted in the Koran as denying his own (and his mother's) divinity. Closely related to this emphasis on the humanity of Jesus is the rejection of the Christian doctrine of the Trinity: it is unbelief to say that God is 'the third of three' (K 5.77), for there is but one God. The Koranic doctrine of Jesus thus establishes a position quite distinct from that of either the Jews, who reject him, or the Christians, who deify him. Here, then, we have a parting of the ways.

It will be evident from this that the Koranic respect for Moses and Jesus does not extend to the bulk of their followers. The Koran does have some friendly things to say of the Christians, despite its strong sense of their fundamental error with regard to the status of their founder. But it also advances a good deal of miscellaneous polemic against them – they consider Mary, the mother of Jesus, to be divine; they hold themselves to be sons of God; they are riven by sectarianism; and so forth.

The Jews receive considerably more attention than the Christians. There is a long appeal to the Children of Israel to fulfil their covenant with God, and to accept Muhammad's message confirming the revelation that had already come to them; some of them would seem to have responded positively. There is a large amount of polemic. Misdeeds of the Biblical Israelites are raked over, such as their worship of the golden calf; the Jews are accused of speaking slanderously of Mary, the mother of Jesus, and are said to be among the most hostile of men towards the true believers. Many of the charges are petty or obscure (e.g. the curious allegation that the Jews consider Ezra to be the son of God), and in general there is more bad feeling towards the Jews than there is towards the Christians. But by contrast, the polemic is not focused on any central issue of doctrine – other than the Jewish refusal to accept Muhammad's own credentials.

Before leaving this stretch of monotheist history, a negative point implicit in all this should be brought out. The Koran is much concerned with the missions of the various monotheist messengers; but it displays little interest in whatever structure of religious authority may have existed in the intervals between these prophetic episodes. Aaron appears in the Koran as the brother of Moses and a participant in the events of his career, but never for his role in the establishment of the Israelite priesthood. The case of the twelve disciples of Jesus is similar: they never figure as the nucleus of the Christian church. Admittedly the Koran has a few things to say about the rabbis and monks of contemporary Judaism and Christianity, and it once mentions Christian priests. It is clear that these figures are thought to have legitimate roles to play in their respective communities; but they tend to be a bad lot, and to be worshipped by their followers in the place of God. One verse refers to monasticism as an institution; it describes it as an innovation of the Christians, not a divinely imposed duty, but does not reject it out of hand. Yet the attention given to these matters is slight.

The role of Arabia

From this survey, it might appear that Arabia played no role in monotheist history until the coming of Muhammad himself. In fact there are two Koranic conceptions which serve to endow Arabia with a monotheist past in its own right; one is rather modest, the other extremely bold.

The first conception is that of the ethnic warner. The idea is that God sends to every people a messenger, usually of their own number, who warns them in their own language to worship God alone; they regularly disregard the warning, and God destroys them in some spectacular fashion. We have already seen the shift of emphasis whereby the Koran presents Noah's career in this light. There is in fact a whole cycle of such stories which appear and reappear in the Koran; what concerns us here is that this stereotype is also extended to Arabia. To take a single example, a certain Salih (a good Arabic name) was sent to Thamud (an attested people of ancient Arabia) with such a message; they ignored it, and were destroyed by a thunderbolt, or some equivalent expression of divine irritation. These Arabian warners are unknown to Jewish or Christian tradition, and their presence in the Koran does something to place Arabia on the monotheist map. But by their very nature, they make no mark on the grand scheme of monotheist history. The episodes are parochial side-shows, and establish no continuing monotheist communities; all that is left is some archaeological remains and a cautionary tale.

The other conception, the 'religion of Abraham', is of a quite different calibre. Its starting-point is the Biblical account of Abraham and his sons. According to the Book of Genesis, Abraham was married to Sarah; but she only bore him a son, Isaac, in their extreme old age. At that time Abraham already had a son, Ishmael, by an Egyptian concubine named Hagar. This had led to considerable ill-feeling between the two women, and already while Hagar was pregnant she had run away into the wilderness. On this occasion an angel had found her by a spring, and sent her home with somewhat qualified promises for the future of her unborn son. When eventually Isaac was born to Sarah, Hagar was sent packing together with her son. This time her water supply ran out, and the child was about to die of thirst when again an angel intervened. Hagar was promised that a great nation would arise from her son, and was miraculously shown a well. Thereafter, we are told, God was with the lad; he grew up in the wilderness and had twelve sons, from whom were descended the twelve Ishmaelite tribes. But for all that, Abraham's heir was Isaac, the ancestor of the Israelites; it was with Isaac, not Ishmael, that God made His everlasting covenant.

The message of this colourful narrative of patriarchal family life is a simple one. Abraham was the common ancestor of the Israelites and the Ishmaelites – or as posterity would put it, of the Jews and the Arabs. Thereafter sacred history was concerned only with the Israelites; the Ishmaelites might be a great nation, but in religious terms they were a dead end.

Much of this picture was accepted by Islam. Muslim scholars thought in the same genealogical idiom, and considered the Arabs (or more precisely, the northern Arabs) to descend from the sons of Ishmael. Equally, as we have seen, Islam accepts the Israelite line of sacred history running from Isaac to Moses and on (in the Christian view) to Jesus. Where Islam departed radically from the Biblical conception was in opening up the Ishmaelite dead end, thereby creating a second line of sacred history that was specifically Arabian.

One Muslim tradition describes the aftermath of the quarrel between Sarah and Hagar. Abraham took Hagar and Ishmael to an uninhabited spot in the wilderness, and left them there. Hagar's water-skin was soon empty, and her child was about to die when Gabriel appeared; he struck the ground with his foot, and a spring gushed forth. The uninhabited spot was Mecca, and the spring was Zamzam, the water-supply of the Meccan sanctuary which we met in connection with

Muhammad's grandfather. Other traditions depart more strongly from the Biblical narrative. God ordered Abraham to build Him a sanctuary where He would be worshipped. Abraham was at first in some perplexity as to how to proceed, but was supernaturally guided to Mecca, accompanied by Hagar and Ishmael. There Abraham and Ishmael built the sanctuary and established the rites of pilgrimage to it. Abraham seems in due course to have departed to resume his Biblical career; but Hagar and Ishmael remained, and at their deaths were buried in the sanctuary. Some say that Ishmael was the first to speak in pure Arabic. He was also a prophet in his own right – and the ancestor of a prophet, Muhammad.

The Arabs thus inherited from their ancestor a monotheist faith and sanctuary. In the course of time, however, this heritage was greatly corrupted. As Mecca became overcrowded with Ishmael's rapidly multiplying descendants, groups of them would move away and subsequently fall into local idolatry. Idols even appeared in the sanctuary itself (Hubal, the most noteworthy, being acquired by a leading Meccan while travelling on business in Moab). In the meantime, the descendants of Ishmael had lost possession of their sanctuary to others, not to regain it till Quraysh settled in Mecca five generations before Muhammad. Yet for all that the Arabs had lapsed into pagan superstition, monotheism remained their birthright.

The elaborate narrative traditions drawn on here are not to be found in the Koran, but the basic conception is present in force. The Koran emphasises that Abraham was a monotheist long before there was such a thing as Judaism or Christianity. 'Abraham was neither a Jew nor a Christian; but he was one of the true religion (*hanif*) who submitted to God (*muslim*)' (K 3.60). That Abraham is here described as, in effect, a Muslim is no surprise; the Koran uses similar language of other monotheists (e.g. Noah, Joseph, the Queen of Sheba, the disciples of Jesus). Its tendency to link the term *muslim* with Abraham in particular is nevertheless a pronounced one. The term *hanif* is also significant. Although its exact sense is obscure, the Koran uses it in contexts suggestive of a pristine monotheism, which it tends to contrast with (latter-day) Judaism and Christianity. It associates the idea strongly with Abraham, but never with Moses or Jesus.

Abraham in turn bequeaths his faith to his sons, warning them to be sure that when they die, they do so in a state of submission to God (*muslim*). He prays that they may not succumb to the worship of idols, and asks God to raise up from his and Ishmael's posterity a people (*umma*) who submit to God (*muslim*). Abraham's religion accordingly remains valid for his descendants. The Koran frequently recommends it, and tells the believers that their religion is that of 'your father Abraham'. (The phrase is to be taken literally; this is not the Christian image of 'our father Abraham' as the *spiritual* ancestor of all believers, whatever their actual descent.) At the same time the story of the building of the sanctuary by Abraham and Ishmael has a prominent place in the Koran; and Abraham speaks of the settlement of some of his posterity in a barren valley beside it (i.e. Mecca).

The effect of these ideas is simple but crucial: they endow Arabia and the Arabs with an honoured place in monotheist history, and one genealogically independent of the Jews and Christians.

The role of Muhammad

The view of sacred history just analysed is in some ways a very consistent one – relentlessly monotheist, and by Biblical standards rather stereotyped. It nevertheless puts side by side two notions between which there is a certain tension. On the one hand there is the conception of a linear succession of monotheist messengers, among whom the founders of Judaism and Christianity find their places. Yet on the other hand we have the idea of an alternative, Arabian monotheism in a line branching off from Abraham. These two conceptions are closely linked to the role, or roles, which the Koran ascribes to Muhammad.

The least adventurous role is that of an ethnic warner. Muhammad's mission is to 'warn the mother of cities (i.e. Mecca) and those round about her' (K 42.5); those to whom he is sent have received no previous warning. The parallel with the earlier ethnic warners is explicit: 'This is a warner, of the warners of old' (K 53.57). This simple conception is a prominent one in the Koran, and each retelling of the cautionary tales about earlier warners helps to underline it. Yet it does not quite fit. For one thing, we find in these passages references to Muhammad as the recipient of a revealed book. Aptly, this scripture is an 'Arabic Koran' – a common Koranic phrase, and a characteristic example of the Koranic emphasis on Arabic as the language of Muhammad's mission. Yet the revelation of a scripture is not a motif that appears in the cautionary tales of earlier warners. And for another thing, Muhammad's people did in the end listen to him, an outcome for which the model of the ethnic warner hardly provided.

A more ambitious conception of Muhammad's role arises out of the religion of Abraham. This pristine monotheism having fallen on evil days, Muhammad could be seen as a messenger sent to restore it. Such a need had been anticipated by Abraham himself. In the course of the major Koranic account of the foundation of the sanctuary, we read that Abraham prayed in these terms on behalf of his descendants: 'Lord, send among them a messenger of their own number who may recite your signs to them, teach them the Book and wisdom, and purify them' (K 2.123). A little later, it is stated that such a messenger has now been sent – a clear reference to Muhammad.

This gives Muhammad a definite position in the structure of monotheist history, and one that goes well with the Arabian setting. But it does not really define his position with regard to the main line of succession, and in particular to Moses and Jesus. It is here that a third conception of Muhammad's role appears. This conception is nicely illustrated in a Koranic sketch of the history of scriptural law: first the Pentateuch was revealed, i.e. to Moses; then Jesus was sent, and to him was revealed the Gospel, confirming the Pentateuch; then the Book (i.e. the Koran) was revealed to Muhammad, confirming what had already been revealed. Conversely, the Koran describes the earlier scriptures as foretelling the coming of Muhammad: he is inscribed in the Pentateuch and the Gospel, and his future mission was part of the good news announced by Jesus. Muhammad is thus authenticated as a new prophet with a new scripture in the direct line of succession to Moses and Jesus.

He is accordingly much more than just a local Arabian prophet. The Koran, after speaking of the endorsement of Muhammad in the Pentateuch and Gospel, goes on to refer to him as 'the messenger of God to you all' (K 7.157); and from this it is but a short step to conceiving him as God's messenger to mankind at large (K 34.27). In practice, as the Koran makes clear, it is not the will of God that mankind should again become the 'one community' they originally were; He guides whom He wills, and by the same token He leads astray whom He wills. But for all the persistence of error, there is now but one true religion for all mankind.

This assertion gains poignancy from the fact that Muhammad is not just the most recent of the prophets, but also the last – the 'seal of the prophets', in a Koranic phrase which has come to be understood in this sense. Tradition has it that Muhammad, comparing his role to those of the earlier prophets, likened himself to the final brick to be laid in the corner of an edifice otherwise completed. His career is accordingly the last major event in monotheist history before the end of the world.

The future

We may end this account with a brief relation of the future course of history as it appeared to early Muslims. This is not a topic treated in the Koran; but it is abundantly (and by no means consistently) treated in early tradition, from which what follows is selected.

The future is nasty, brutish and short. The Muslim community will break up into a mass of conflicting sects, just as the Children of Israel had done before them. Sedition will follow sedition like strips of the darkest night, and the living will envy the dead. Eventually God will send a redeemer, a descendant of Muhammad. This redeemer, the Mahdi, will receive allegiance at the sanctuary in Mecca, whence his emigration (*hijra*) will be to Jerusalem; there he will reign in justice. Yet this interlude will last less than a decade. Thereafter Antichrist (the Dajjal) will appear from Iraq, reducing the Muslims to a remnant making their last stand on the peak of a mountain in Syria. In the hour of their need, Jesus will descend to earth in armour and lead them against Antichrist, slaying him at the gate of Lydda in Palestine; then Jesus will reign in justice and plenty, exterminating the pig and breaking the crosses of the Christians. Yet this too will pass, giving way to the final horrors of human history. At the last a wind takes up the souls of the believers, the sun rises in the west, and history gives way to the cataclysmic eschatology of the Koran.

41

5 Monotheist law

The Koranic view of history is in some ways rather repetitive. Successive messengers arrive with the same doctrinal message. There is, however, a certain ringing of changes with regard to the outward form and precise content of the messages. Sometimes they are in writing; sometimes, apparently, they are not. What is more, the various revealed books, while of course confirming each other in general terms, may differ significantly in points of detail. God tells Muhammad that 'to every term there is a book' (K 13.38), that is, each age has its scripture; in it God erases or confirms what He ·pleases, the 'mother of the Book' (presumably a kind of archetype) being with Him. In other words, the content of revelation is liable to change from one prophetic epoch to another.

The field in which this instability is most marked is divine law – law which God Himself makes and unmakes. To each community God assigned its particular way; thus each has its own way of slaughtering (or sacrificing) animals, and yet 'their God is one god' (K 22.35). Whereas the truth of monotheist doctrine is timeless, the validity of monotheist law is a more relative matter. Even within the Koran itself, the Muslim scholars found scriptural support for the view that earlier verses could be abrogated by later ones.

Law before the Koran

The pivotal event in the Koranic view of the history of law is the revelation of the Pentateuch to Moses. There is little indication that law played much part in God's dealings with mankind before this event. We learn incidentally that God had revealed the duties of prayer and almsgiving to Abraham, Isaac and Jacob, and that Ishmael imposed them on his family; but for the most part Abrahamic law remains as shadowy as the scripture with which the Koran occasionally endows him. With Moses, we are on firmer ground. The Pentateuch contains the 'judgement of God', and by it the Prophets judged the Jews. Some of its concrete legal stipulations are cited – a couple of dietary laws, for example, and the principle of 'a life for a life'. The Pentateuch (or the set of tablets which God gave to Moses) deals fully with all questions; in it are guidance and light.

There is nevertheless a strong sense in the Koran that the yoke of the Pentateuchal code was an unduly heavy one, and that this, though God's responsibility, is the fault of the Jews. This idea finds clear expression with regard to dietary law. The Koran insists that dietary prohibitions of divine origin were first introduced in the Pentateuch: 'Every food was lawful to the Children of Israel, except what Israel (i.e. Jacob) forbade to himself, before the revelation of the Pentateuch' (K 3.87). That God then forbade to the Israelites foods previously permitted to them was a punishment for their own misdeeds.

The tendency since the revelation of the Pentateuch has accordingly been for God to ease the yoke of the law. The mission of Jesus is conceived in a manner rather similar to that of Moses, in the sense that the scripture revealed to him, the Gospel, is a law-book according to which his followers are to be judged. Yet at the same time it is part of his mission 'to declare lawful to you some of what was forbidden to you' (K 3.44). Muhammad's role is similarly conceived, and is perhaps thought of as going further in the direction of liberalisation. Much, of course, is carried over from earlier dispensations; thus the obligation to fast is laid upon the believers 'as it was laid upon those who were before you' (K 2.179). Dietary law, however, is drastically pruned: the prohibitions are reduced to a few key points, and these provisions are expressly contrasted with the more elaborate restrictions which God had imposed on the Jews. The case of the Sabbath is similar. Without question it had been imposed on the Jews, and one verse which was to cause a considerable theological flurry tells how God metamorphosed Sabbath-breakers into apes. Yet this did not mean that the Sabbath was binding on Muhammad's own community. It had been imposed only on 'those who differed concerning it' (presumably the Jews), and – so the context seems to imply – forms no part of the religion of Abraham.

Historically, this Koranic perspective on the history of law is in some ways an apt one. Law was a late starter in religious history. The gods of the ancient Near East did not usually concern themselves with legislation, and law was not a central feature of the culture of their priests. The salience of law in ancient Israelite religion was thus unusual – and still more so the later elaboration of the Biblical heritage into the law-centred culture of the Jewish rabbis. It is also legitimate to think of a trend towards liberalisation, and to place both Jesus and Muhammad within it. Yet there is a fundamental difference here which the Koran, in bringing Jesus firmly into line between Moses and Muhammad, has glossed over. The Gospel is not a law-book. Its message is rather that the Law is not enough; and the followers of Jesus soon went on to infer that most of it was not necessary at all. The dietary code of the Pentateuch still stands in the Christian Bible as 'appointed to be read in churches', but it would be bizarre, indeed sinful, for Christians to observe it. Christianity, in short, is not a law-centred religion. Islam, for all its liberalisation, unmistakably remains one, and in this it is supported by the legal content of the Koran.

Koranic law

In the early Islamic period there was a school of thought which saw the Koran as the sole and sufficient basis of Islamic law. God Himself, it was argued, describes the Koran as a book which makes everything clear. The consensus of Muslim scholars, however, was against this view. Too much is left unsaid in the Koran; for example, it tells the believer to pray, but omits essential information as to how he should do it. The bulk of Islamic law as it actually evolved is thus non-Koranic in substance. Some of what is missing is supplied from the innumerable traditions regarding the sayings and doings of Muhammad. A typical example of such a tradition was given in Chapter 2: at the conquest of Khaybar, Muhammad is said to have declared the eating of the flesh of the domesticated ass forbidden. At the same time, the lawyers had to rely, in one way or another, on their own legal reasoning. All this would bulk large in any survey of Islamic law as such; here, however, I shall focus on such law as there is in the Koran.

Although it does not add up to a comprehensive law-code, the Koranic treatment of law covers a wide range of subject-matter. In the first place, it deals with specifically religious rituals and duties: washing, prayer, almsgiving, fasting, and pilgrimage to the sanctuary. The treatment is uneven; thus the instructions on the fast are fairly full, whereas no indication is given as to how much alms a believer should give. It is nonetheless clear from the way in which the topics are treated that God's interest as a lawgiver is not confined to generalities. For example, the believer in preparing himself for prayer is specifically instructed to wash his arms up to the *elbows*, and to wipe his feet to the *ankles*. In the second place, the Koran discusses a range of less narrowly religious aspects of law: marriage, divorce, inheritance, homicide, theft, usury, the drinking of wine, and the like. Again, the treatment is uneven: thieves are to be punished by having their hands cut off, but the fate of the unrepentant usurer is not prescribed (though he receives a dire warning that he will find himself at war with God and His messenger). The scope and character of this material suffices to define Islam as a legally oriented religion.

A more concrete sense of the nature of Koranic law can best be gained from examples. I shall accordingly outline what the Koran has to say on three specific legal topics: the rites of pilgrimage, dietary restrictions, and the status of women.

1. The Koran gives considerable attention to the rites of pilgrimage, yet what it has to say is not intelligible as it stands; I shall accordingly supply in brackets a minimum of non-Koranic material from early sources. We can best begin with the layout of the sanctuary in its widest sense. We have already encountered the Ka'ba. (This is the cubic building towards which Muslims pray; in one corner is set a black stone of peculiar sanctity.) To it we must now add (working outwards from Mecca): Safa and Marwa (two hillocks within a few hundred yards of the Ka'ba); an unnamed place of sacrifice (at Mina, a few miles from Mecca); the 'holy waymark' (Muzdalifa, a couple of miles further out); and 'Arafat (a hill located twelve miles out of Mecca). We shall encounter these places in reverse order.

The main form of pilgrimage is that known as the *hajj*. Its performance (once in a lifetime) is a duty for those able to undertake it. It takes place (annually) in the holy month (of Dhu 'l-Hijja). Three main components of the rites are referred to in an unambiguous fashion in the Koran. (There are of course others, including the central rite of the entire pilgrimage: the pilgrims go out to 'Arafat and wait there till sunset.) The Koranic rites are: (i) The pilgrims (then) 'rush' from 'Arafat (to Muzdalifa, the 'holy waymark'); they then again 'rush' from the 'holy waymark' (i.e. from Muzdalifa to Mina). (ii) They sacrifice (at Mina, whereupon they shave their heads before proceeding to Mecca itself). (iii) They then circumambulate 'the ancient house' (i.e. the Kaʻba). (They do this seven times, if possible kissing or touching the black stone. In fact pilgrims are likely to have performed this ceremony once before, on first arriving in Mecca before going out to ʻArafat.) If they want, they can also circumambulate Safa and Marwa. (Thereafter, there are further but less arduous rites back at Mina.)

During the *hajj* the pilgrims are in a special ritual state (which they leave by stages towards the end of the rites). They may not hunt, though they may fish. They must abstain from quarrelsome behaviour and lascivious talk (such as telling a woman one's intentions towards her when the pilgrimage is over). (In fact sexual relations are excluded altogether; at the same time the pilgrims wear special clothing, and may not cut their hair or nails, or use perfume.)

Two points are worth noting about the entire ritual complex. The first is that the rites, though physically demanding, are simple; there is little that cannot be done by the ordinary believer who knows his religious duties. (Even the sacrifice at Mina, where one might have expected some kind of priesthood to be at work, is performed by the pilgrims themselves.) The second point is that the meaning of the rituals is more than a little opaque, and that the Koran shows little disposition to interpret them. Why 'rush'? and why spend so much of a visit to God's house in a set of locations several miles from it?

2. As we have seen, the Koran takes an interest in the place of dietary prohibitions in the history of monotheist law. This is no accident; dietary law as it appears in the Koran is a thoroughly contentious issue. There is frequent polemic against those who falsely ascribe dietary regulations to God.

Devils are at work inspiring their friends to dispute with the believers, and troublemakers are engaged in leading people astray. The malice of the troublemakers consists in alleging that God has prohibited foods which are in fact perfectly lawful. (This, incidentally, is surprising in an Arabian context; historically one might have expected it to be the other way round.) Accordingly, the believers are repeatedly urged to eat the good things which God has given them, and are not to declare them forbidden. No sin accrues to an honest believer on account of what he eats; or more exactly, God has spelt out those few things that are in fact forbidden, leaving no ground for misplaced zeal in dietary matters.

As this suggests, the Koran tends to list forbidden rather than permitted foods. Its concern, as will appear, is always with meat; vegetarians have no problems other than the prohibition of wine, which does not concern us here. We can consider the Koranic rulings under two heads.

First, what animals are forbidden as such? The only one named is the pig; cattle – in a wide sense – are expressly permitted. (Does God then intend to allow the eating of hares, shellfish, lizards and mermaids? Such questions received much attention, and a variety of answers, from the Muslim scholars.)

Second, in what ways can the meat of a permitted animal become forbidden? The implicit but fundamental point is that animals have to be slaughtered in a proper ritual fashion (though fish and locusts were generally considered an exception to this). Thus carrion is forbidden, as is the victim of a beast of prey, or an animal killed by strangling; again implicit here is the principle that the mode of slaughter must shed the animal's blood, the eating of blood as such being expressly forbidden. More specifically religious is the prohibition of meat consecrated to (gods) other than God, or sacrificed on pagan altars; this in fact extends to whatever has not had the name of God invoked over it (i.e. as part of the ritual of slaughter). On the other hand, there is no objection to 'the food of those to whom the Book was brought' (K 5.7). (This clearly refers to Jews and Christians. Presumably 'food' includes meat; so at least the scholars of Sunni Islam have held, though others have denied it.)

The Koran regularly adds to its lists of forbidden foods an assurance that these provisions can be overridden in cases of dire need. It is better to eat carrion than to starve.

3. The status of women is extensively treated in the Koran. God's views on this matter are on the whole unfashionable at the present day. Women are not equal, and are to be beaten if they get out of hand. As in ancient Israel, polygamy and concubinage are allowed, and women are easily divorced; with regard to the extent of polygamy, the Koran speaks of believers taking two, three or four wives. (But with the single exception of Muhammad himself, they may not take more.) Within this framework, there is a good deal of provision intended to secure the decent treatment of women. For example, there is compulsory financial provision for widows for a year after the death of the husband; and men are advised, politely but firmly, that when they die their widows will have every right to remarry after a specified interval. Women are also accorded a significant place in the inheritance system; they receive shares – generally at half the corresponding male rate – in the estates of their parents and near relatives.

Other provisions are concerned with the problems of ritual purity and public decency to which the existence of women gives rise. Thus men are enjoined to separate themselves from menstruating women. (By sleeping in separate beds? or in the same bed but with separate sheets? or simply by abstaining from full intercourse? Here, as often, God's words left the scholars with much to discuss; on this question they tended to a liberal view.) When in public, women should cover their bosoms (the Koran does not mention their faces). The punishment for adultery is a public flogging for both parties; it takes four witnesses to prove such a charge. (There is no mention of stoning in the Koran as we have it, though Muhammad is said to have inflicted this penalty on adulterers when the issue was forced on him.)

The general question to which these examples give rise is the sense in which Koranic law is monotheist. In a basic way, much of it is not, in the sense that there is little about its actual content which is *intrinsically* monotheist. What the Koran has to say of the status of women does not follow from the postulate that God is one, and could just as well be conjoined with polytheism or atheism. This is also true for much of the concrete detail of dietary law, with the exception of the provisions regarding the religious aegis under which an animal can validly be slaughtered. The case of pilgrimage is different, since it is a form of worship; and those aspects of the ritual which are performed around the Ka'ba have a strong monotheist association, inasmuch as this sanctuary was appointed by God and established by His prophet Abraham. With other aspects of the ritual, however, the association is a good deal looser. In general, what is monotheist about Koranic law is not its content but its form – not what God says, but the fact that it is He who says it.

6 Monotheist politics

The traditional biography of Muhammad presents his career as a remarkable combination of religion and politics, and this combination can fairly be seen as the key to his success. As we saw, he made little headway as a prophet until he became a successful politician; but at the same time, his political opportunity turned on his credentials as a prophet. His religion and his politics were not two separate activities that came to be entangled; they were fused together, and this fusion was expressed doctrinally in the distinctive vocabulary of monotheist politics that pervades the Koran. The theme of this vocabulary is quite literally revolution, the triumph of the believers against the pervasive oppression of unbelief.

The oppressed

From the numerous Koranic references to the oppression to which believers are exposed, we may pick out one particularly evocative term: *mustad'af*. Literally it means 'deemed weak'; an apt translation might be 'underdog', but here I shall settle for the less colourful rendering 'oppressed'. Like the rest of the terms to be discussed in this chapter, it is a loaded one; and like most of them, it is not confined to the context of Muhammad's own career. Striking examples of its use are to be found in the Koranic versions of the story of Moses and Pharaoh. Here Pharaoh's iniquities include oppressing a section of the population (i.e. the Israelites). God, however, wishes an end to this injustice: 'We desire to be gracious to those who have been oppressed in the land,. . . to make them the inheritors, and to establish them in the land' (K 28.4–5);

and in due course His promise comes true. Here, then, the term identifies a group whose very wretchedness in the present marks them out for future deliverance. It is similarly applied in the context of Muhammad's own career. God reminds his followers – now home and dry – that they had once been 'few, oppressed in the land' (K 8.26), but that He had then given them refuge and come to their aid.

The situation of the oppressed is thus one which can engage some divine sympathy, but in itself it is not enough. It will not excuse spineless resignation. This point is dramatised in Koranic accounts of the day of judgement when all unbelievers get their deserts. The weak among the unbelievers will then try to blame the strong: they were oppressed, they say, and only followed their oppressors in unbelief. Yet this whining will avail them nothing. A clue to what they might have done to escape their predicament is suggested by a prayer which the Koran places in the mouths of the oppressed in relation to Muhammad's mission: 'lead us out from this city of oppressors' (K 4.77). The moral is to get up and go. It is expressed with some brutality by angels who in one passage engage in dialogue with the souls of certain people who are contemptuously described as having 'wronged themselves'. The angels ask for their account, and receive the plaintive reply: 'We were oppressed in the land.' To this the angels retort: 'Was God's earth not wide enough for you to emigrate somewhere else in it?' (K 4.99).

Hijra

The word for 'emigrate' used by the angels derives from a root we have already met in the terms *hijra* and *muhajirun*. The Koran does not, as it happens, make use of the noun *hijra* to refer to the act of emigration, or apply the notion to Muhammad himself; but the participle *muhajirun*, and related verbal forms, are frequently applied to his followers. Thus the Koran speaks of those who emigrated after being oppressed or persecuted, and of those who emigrate 'in the way of God', leaving their homes behind them. There are numerous promises that God will reward such emigrants. Sometimes their departure is presented as a matter of expulsion rather than choice, but it is always construed as a positive act. It is also tantamount to joining Muhammad's community. Those who merely believe, but have yet to emigrate, have little or no claim on its loyalty.

As it happens, the Koran does not use the term in the context of the Mosaic exodus from Egypt. It does, however, apply it in an Abrahamic context, where it seems to be Abraham himself who declares: 'I am an emigrant (*muhajir*) unto my Lord' (K 29.25). The reference is presumably to his separation from his idolatrous people and his journey to the Holy Land, and the term thus acquires a place in the 'religion of Abraham'.

Jihad

We saw in Chapter 2 how tradition presents the *hijra* as the turning-point of Muhammad's career. In Mecca his role had been confined to calling people to God, and he had been obliged to endure patiently the maltreatment to which this exposed him. But shortly before the *hijra*, a verse was revealed to him permitting him to make war and shed blood: 'Permission is granted to those who fight because they have been wronged. God is well able to come to their aid – those who have been driven out of their homes unjustly' (K 22.40). Soon afterwards, Muhammad emigrated, and from Medina he was able to avail himself of the new permission to good effect. In itself, of course, emigration did not have to lead to war; those of Muhammad's followers who had previously emigrated to

Ethiopia in what came to be known as the 'first *hijra*' had been peaceful refugees. In Muhammad's case the link was nevertheless a strong one, and the Koran often refers in one breath to emigration and war.

War against the unbelievers (*jihad*, literally 'effort') is accordingly a prominent theme in the Koran. God not only permits it, He orders it to be waged till His cause prevails. Not all injunctions on the subject are as aggressive as this; there are indications that the unbelievers should be left to start the war, and that hostilities may be terminated or interrupted by peace agreements. In the case of Jews and Christians, honour is satisfied if they pay tribute. Yet the general atmosphere is one of enthusiasm. Although not everybody is obliged to participate in the war, the lukewarm are strongly encouraged to do so. Those who go out and fight will earn from God a far greater reward than those who sit at home. Twenty steadfast believers will defeat two hundred unbelievers, and a hundred will overcome a thousand. (The next verse, however, revises these ratios in a less optimistic direction.) Those killed in the war should not be spoken of as dead: even now they are alive. They have struck a bargain with God: 'God has bought from the believers their selves and their substance in return for Paradise; they fight in the way of God, killing and being killed. . . Who is more true to his covenant than God?' (K 9.112). At the same time, God's intimate involvement is emphasised by His practical aid on the battlefield. At Badr, where God gave Muhammad and his followers victory, He reinforced them with an army of angels, and on other occasions he sent to their aid 'armies you did not see'. That this is holy war is likewise evident in the way in which its needs can override other religious values. Thus fighting in the sacred month is pronounced an evil, but of less weight than the evil the war is directed against.

As might be expected, the Koran refers to religious war in earlier contexts of monotheist history. It appears as a religious duty in ancient Israel in an account of the establishment of the monarchy – though the performance of the Israelites as described here is unimpressive, as it had also been when Moses had called upon his people to enter the promised land. Other prophets seem to have been better served; there were numerous prophets for whom myriads fought unflinchingly against the unbelievers, to be rewarded for it in both this world and the next. An aspect of religious war which is not mentioned in earlier contexts is the division of the spoils; this is a matter to which the Koran devotes some attention, and tradition has Muhammad declare himself the first prophet to whom booty was made lawful.

Alongside the war against the unbelievers without, the Koran also reflects a struggle against the hypocrites (*munafiqun*) within the community. Though they had accepted Muhammad's message, they harboured unbelief in their hearts. They were lazy in performing the duty of prayer, sceptical about Muhammad's revelations, politically unreliable, and destined (some slight hopes of repentance apart) for eternal punishment in the lowest level of hell. One passage envisages a definitive break with them, after which they will be liable to be taken and killed wherever they are found; and in others, Muhammad is told to fight them – and the unbelievers at large – without remorse. The phenomenon of hypocrisy does not explicitly appear in the Koran as one which earlier prophets had to contend with.

The umma

Unlike the 'first *hijra*' to Ethiopia, Muhammad's emigration led to the creation of a politically autonomous community. This emerges most clearly in a document transmitted by tradition which we have already encountered, the 'Constitution of Medina'. It is there declared that 'the believers and Muslims of Quraysh and Yathrib, and those who follow them, join them and fight alongside them' are 'one community (*umma*) to the exclusion of all other people' (S 231-2). They are to stand united against whatever troublemakers appear in their midst; they are to be mutual friends (the term has a more political connotation than this English rendering carries); and any serious dispute is to be referred to God and Muhammad. In short, the document constitutes a community and designates an authority within it.

Much of this picture can also be elicited from the Koran. The believers are told not to take unbelievers rather than other believers as friends. Muhammad's followers and helpers are affirmed to be friends one of another. There are frequent demands for obedience to 'God and His messenger', and the believers are instructed that 'if you quarrel about anything, refer it to God and the messenger' (K 4.62).

It would be a mistake to see this community as an egalitarian one. Human inequality is a common theme in the Koran, both inside and outside the community. Yet if we leave aside the inferior status of women and slaves, the Koran endorses no inequalities among the believers other than those of religious merit. Thus it emphasises that those who do not participate in holy war cannot be considered the equals of those who do, and asserts generally that 'the noblest among you in the sight of God is the most godfearing' (K 49.13). But there is nothing here to underwrite a privileged position for an aristocracy or priesthood, and the political atmosphere is strikingly lacking in pomp and ceremony. Muhammad is told that he should take counsel with the believers when problems arise; the believers are instructed not to raise their voices above that of the Prophet, and not to shout at him in the way they

shout at each other. It is of a piece with this immediate relationship between Muhammad and his community that
neither Koran nor tradition speaks of any formal and continuing structure of authority interposing between them.
(Contrast the elaborate hierarchy of administrators of tens,
hundreds etc. which the Bible tells us was established by
Moses to take routine matters off his hands.) There are
intermediate powers only where Muhammad himself is not
present, as when he appoints commanders of expeditions,
governors of distant tribes, or a temporary deputy during an
absence from Medina.

Taken together, these ideas suggest a simple and powerful
model of political action against the oppression of an
unbelieving society. The remedy for the victims is in the first
instance to emigrate. This in turn leads to the creation of a
new and autonomous polity, the act of emigration placing
both physical and moral distance between the old and the
new. The new community then embarks on a remorseless
struggle against its enemies, the unbelievers without and the
hypocrites within. The monotheist context of these notions
gives them force and definition. There is only one God, and
men are either His friends or His enemies. 'Now is the way of
truth manifestly distinguished from error ... God is the
friend of the believers, bringing them out of darkness into
light; but the friends of the unbelievers are idols, who bring
them out of light into darkness' (K 2.257-9). Manifest distinction is but a step from armed confrontation: 'The believers
fight in the way of God, the unbelievers in the way of idols; so
fight the friends of Satan!' (K 4.78). Then assuredly the
oppressors will know 'by what overturning they will be
overturned' (K 26.228).

These ideas are not notably eirenic, and to anyone brought

up on the New Testament they will seem very alien. In the face of persecution, Jesus neither resisted nor emigrated. He created no new polity, at least not in this world, he waged no holy wars, and he gave a most evasive answer when after his resurrection his followers suggested that the time might have come to 'restore again the kingdom to Israel' (Acts, 1.6). If Christians want to be political activists, they cannot in good faith take their values from the life of their founder.

Muhammad has a good deal more in common with Moses, an altogether less dovish Biblical figure. The story of Moses tells of a people who lived in bondage in Egypt, were led out by their God and His prophet amid scenes of fearsome devastation, and went on to live a nomadic life in the wilderness in preparation for the conquest of the land God had promised them – a conquest eventually achieved with no small amount of slaughter. Here, then, is politics in a style more akin to Muhammad's.

There is nevertheless a significant difference of idiom. The Biblical account of the exodus, the wanderings and the conquest identifies the peoples involved in ordinary ethnic terms. The people whom Moses leads out of Egypt are the 'Children of Israel', and remain so irrespective of whether they worship God or the golden calf. Their enemies are referred to in the same way: Egyptians, Amorites, Perizzites and so forth. The Koran, by contrast, is not given to speaking in this manner; its categories are ideological rather than descriptive. God's people are 'those who submit' to Him, 'those who believe', 'the friends of God'; against them are ranged 'the hypocrites', 'the unbelievers', 'the polytheists', 'the enemies of God', 'the friends of Satan'. Terms like *muhajirun* and *jihad* are similarly ideological; they have no parallel in the Biblical narratives, which use the same commonplace vocabulary to describe the comings, goings and battles of all and sundry. In short, the

Bible does no more than tell a story of monotheist politics, whereas the Koran might be said to provide something approximating to a theory.

What this theory meant for posterity is a question that can only be touched on here. It takes no great insight to see that Muhammad's tribal polity was in some ways an anomalous paradigm for the world that resulted from the very success of Islam – a vast territory populated mainly by peasants, and dominated by cities and states such as Arabia had never seen. Under such conditions the Muslims could no longer function politically as the single community they had once been, and the nature of the Muslim state had undergone drastic change. As part of a doctrinal adaptation to these altered circumstances, key notions of Muhammad's politics were widely held no longer to apply; in the mainstream of Sunni Islam the view was thus usually taken that the duty of *hijra* had ceased when Muhammad conquered Mecca. Yet there remained Muslims who engaged in vigorous re-enactments of his ideas, often in tribal environments akin to his own, and several of Muhammad's notions are very much alive at the present day.

This chapter, and the preceding one, have emphasised how much in the life of Muhammad's followers is subject to divine norms. This does not, however, mean that all human action without exception is subject to direct prescription by God, and that no scope is left for purely human choices. The point is nicely dramatised in an exchange which tradition describes between Muhammad and a certain Hubab shortly before the battle of Badr. When Muhammad had halted his troops, he was accosted by Hubab, who asked: 'Prophet, this position we've taken up, is it one revealed to you by God from which we can neither move forward nor back, or is it just a matter of judgement and tactics?' When Muhammad replied that it was a purely tactical matter, Hubab went on to give him some advice: 'Prophet, this isn't the right place to be. Get everyone moving so we reach the water-supply closest to the enemy.' Muhammad promptly did so, depriving the enemy of water, and won the battle (S 296–7). Even believers do not attain victory simply by being on the side of the angels.

7 The sources

Two rather different types of source-material have been drawn on in the preceding chapters: Koran and tradition. The Koran is a scripture with a fixed content and – within narrow limits – an invariant text. Tradition is more amorphous. It is whatever the Muslim scholars have handed down, formally by a process of oral transmission, in practice as a vast literature. It embraces all aspects of the sayings and doings of early Muslims, and comprises many different genres; within it a particular tradition may recur in a variety of contexts and in numerous variants. The early narrative accounts of the life of Muhammad form a small if significant part of this body of material, and it is with them that we can best begin a closer look at our sources.

The narrative sources

We possess a fair number of works of scholarship written in the ninth century or so which include, often within some larger framework, accounts of Muhammad's life. These works are not free literary compositions. Their authors were compilers who drew on a mass of earlier literature which is otherwise mostly lost. Good Muslim compilers are responsible scholars who tell us to whom they owe their materials, and thereby enable us to reconstruct something of the sources they were using. There are, however, limits to this reconstruction. The rules of the game allow the compiler a freedom of wording in reproducing his source which may be considerable, and do not oblige him either to quote in full or to indicate his omissions. Since he normally quotes in units of a few lines to a couple of pages, and then frequently switches to a different source, we may be left pretty much in the dark as to the overall structure of his sources. Moreover, the conventions of transmission require that the compiler quote men, not books; whether the authority in question had in fact written on the subject, or is merely a source of oral information, is not usually apparent from the way in which the compiler refers to him.

A partial exception to these remarks is Ibn Hisham (d. 833). What he did was to confine himself to the work of one and only one of his predecessors, Ibn Ishaq (d. 767). More precisely, he edited that portion of Ibn Ishaq's work which dealt with the life of Muhammad, using the version transmitted to him by one of his teachers. Yet he too proceeded by quoting his material in the customary blocks; and he was scrupulous enough to warn his readers in general terms that he had omitted a good many things from a variety of motives. We also possess a considerable volume of citations from Ibn Ishaq in sources independent of Ibn Hisham. An unusually deviant body of such material bearing on the early period of Muhammad's life has recently been published, and brings home both the extent of Ibn Hisham's omissions, and the difficulty at any given point of reconstructing the exact words of Ibn Ishaq. Yet if our image of Ibn Ishaq's work is blurred, and likely to remain so, we still know a great deal about it, and it is on this basis that at several points in this book I have referred without hesitation to Ibn Ishaq as having said this or that.

Ibn Ishaq's biography of Muhammad, though in the long run easily the most successful, was far from being the only one produced in his day. For example, we possess a shorter and simpler biography which may stem from the scholar Ma'mar ibn Rashid (d. 770), and which is preserved for us in the same kind of way as Ibn Ishaq's work. Further biographies were written in the second half of the eighth century. We may perhaps include here the work of Waqidi (d. 823); a large part of it survives, and what is lost is represented by extensive quotations.

At some point in this discussion we have to descend to detail, and comparing Waqidi with his predecessors is an instructive way to do it. Let us take a point which in itself is quite trivial: when and how did 'Abdallah, the father of Muhammad, die? Ibn Ishaq tells us that 'Abdallah died while his wife was pregnant with Muhammad – though in one line of transmission a statement has been added to the effect that he may rather have died when Muhammad was twenty-eight months old, and that God knows best which is right. Ma'mar likewise (if we take the account he transmits to be essentially his own) has 'Abdallah die while Muhammad is still in the womb, and is able to give a short account of the circumstances: 'Abdallah had been sent by his own father, 'Abd al-Muttalib, to lay in stores of dates in Yathrib, and died there. Two further scholars of this generation are quoted by a ninth-century compiler for the view that 'Abdallah died when Muhammad was twenty-eight months old, or perhaps it was seven. The conclusion to be drawn from this range of opinions is obvious: the scholars of the first half of the eighth century were agreed that 'Abdallah had died early enough to leave Muhammad an orphan; but as to the details, God knew best.

By the later eighth century times had changed, and it was Waqidi who knew best. Waqidi knew that 'Abdallah had gone to Gaza on business, had fallen ill on the way back, and died in Yathrib after leaving the caravan he was with to be nursed by relations there. Waqidi was further able to specify 'Abdallah's age at death and the exact place of his burial. Naturally he also knew when the event took place, namely while Muhammad was still in the womb. He was aware that this was not the only account of the matter, but pronounced it the best. This evolution in the course of half a century from uncertainty to profusion of precise detail is an instructive one. It suggests that a fair amount of what Waqidi knew was not knowledge. Similar effects have been demonstrated in Waqidi's treatment of the course and chronology of much later events in the biography of Muhammad.

What kind of sources lie behind the works of Ibn Ishaq and his generation? Since most of the research in this field remains to be done, I shall proceed here by setting out two contrasting positions; my own sympathies lie with the second.

Our starting-point is the fact that the writers of Ibn Ishaq's day are in the habit of naming their sources, just as the ninth-century compilers do. Often they give a whole chain of such sources reaching back to an eyewitness of the event in question, and for one event we may be able to collect several accounts going back through distinct chains to different eyewitnesses. Such chains of authorities (*isnad*s, as they are called) are in fact a salient characteristic of Muslim tradition in general. A legal ruling of Muhammad, or an interpretation of a Koranic verse by one of his leading followers, will be quoted with such a chain, and a spurious tradition will be equipped with a spurious chain.

Two questions now arise in connection with our narrative sources. First, how far are the chains of authorities to be taken as genuine? Second, are we to take it that the authorities named in these chains were (like Ibn Ishaq and his likes) the authors of books?

One view, which does not lack for adherents, is that the chains are genuine and the authorities are authors. Thus we can simply extend back the kind of reconstruction that works for the biographies of Ibn Ishaq's day. For example, he and his contemporaries make frequent reference to Zuhri (d. 742), a major figure of the previous generation. An energetic researcher could then collect all the quotations relating to the life of Muhammad that are given on Zuhri's authority, and hope to emerge with something like a reconstruction of his work. It would of course have to be conceded that the further back we go, the more blurred our reconstructions are likely to become. But this is a small price to pay for the overall assurance of the reliability of our sources. If these sources preserve for us a literature that reaches back to the contemporaries of Muhammad, and if they preserve the testimony of numerous mutually independent witnesses, then there is little room for the sceptic in the study of Muhammad's life.

The other view is that false ascription was rife among the eighth-century scholars, and that in any case Ibn Ishaq and his contemporaries were drawing on oral tradition. Neither of these propositions is as arbitrary as it sounds. We have reason to believe that numerous traditions on questions of dogma and law were provided with spurious chains of authorities by those who put them into circulation; and at the same time we have much evidence of controversy in the eighth century as to whether it was permissible to reduce oral tradition to writing. The implications of this view for the reliability of our sources are clearly rather negative. If we cannot trust the chains of authorities, we can no longer claim to know that we have before us the separately transmitted accounts of independent witnesses; and if knowledge of the life of Muhammad was transmitted orally for a century before it was reduced to writing, then the chances are that the material will have undergone considerable alteration in the process.

Which of these positions, or what middle course, lies closest to the truth is something which – to borrow the idiom of the Muslim scholars – God knows best. Thus to return for a minute to Zuhri, the sources are bewilderingly inconsistent about his literary activity: we are told that he was a prolific writer who wrote down all the traditions he heard, and we are told that he never wrote anything at all, and left no book behind him. Setting side by side quotations from Zuhri given in different sources produces, in my own experience, similarly inconsistent results; and sometimes one finds striking verbal similarities between two versions of an event ascribed to Zuhri, only to encounter the same echoes in versions ascribed to quite different authorities.

The most interesting hypothesis which has been advanced, and one which accounts rather well for this and other effects, is that the eighth-century authors drew much of their material directly from the specialist story-tellers of early Islam, the *qussas*. We should then think in terms of a common repertoire of material in circulation among these story-tellers, rather than of hard and fast lines of individual transmission. If, as is plausible, we assume that this story-telling remained a living source for the authors of scholarly biographies as late as the time of Waqidi, we can readily explain Waqidi's superior knowledge as a reflection of the continuing evolution of this oral tradition.

Story-telling is an art, not a science, and signs of this art are commonplace in the biography of Muhammad. For example, one element in the repertoire was clearly a story of a frightening encounter between the woman who suckled the infant Muhammad and some person or persons whose spiritual expertise enabled them to divine his future greatness. Whether the encounter is with Jews, Ethiopian Christians, or an Arab soothsayer, is nevertheless a point which varies from one version of the story to another. Similar floating anecdotes occur later in Muhammad's life. The details again are trivial, but the overall implications are not. We have seen what half a century of story-telling could achieve between Ibn Ishaq and Waqidi, at a time when we know that much material had already been committed to writing. What the same processes may have brought about in the century before Ibn Ishaq is something we can only guess at.

In this situation, how is the historian to proceed? The usual practice is to accept whatever in the sources we lack specific reason to reject. This may be the right approach; doubtless there is a historical core to the tradition on Muhammad's life, and perhaps a little judicious selectivity is enough to uncover it. Yet it may equally be the case that we are nearer the mark in rejecting whatever we do not have specific reason to accept, and that what is usually taken for bedrock is no more than shifting sand. We can best pursue the question when we have first discussed the Koran.

The Koran

Tradition describes Muhammad as receiving his revelations bit by bit, and this seems to find support in some (though not all) of the relevant Koranic statements. As we now have them, however, Muhammad's revelations are in the form of a book. There is a rich body of traditions as to how the Koran was collected and edited to yield the text we have today, and two points are more or less common ground: that the task was not accomplished by Muhammad himself, and that it was completed at the latest in the reign of the Caliph 'Uthman (ruled 644–56). This apart, the traditions are not a model of consistency. We learn that some of Muhammad's followers already knew the whole Koran by heart in his lifetime – yet subsequently it had to be pieced together out of fragments collected from here and there. We are told that Muhammad regularly dictated his revelations to a scribe – yet the scripture was later in danger of being lost through the death in battle of those who had it by heart. It was collected and made into a book by the first Caliph; or by the second; or by the third, 'Uthman. Alternatively, it had already been collected before the time of 'Uthman, and he merely had the text standardised and other versions destroyed. The last of these traditions has tended to prevail, but the choice is a somewhat arbitrary one; the truth may lie anywhere within the limits of the discordant traditions, or altogether outside them.

Turning to the book itself, its structure needs some elucidation. Outwardly it is clear enough: like the Bible, the Koran comes in chapters (*sura*s) and verses (*aya*s) – though not 'books'. The verses often rhyme, but they are not the verses of poetry. The *sura*s are composed of anything from three to nearly three hundred verses apiece, and are arranged in roughly descending order of length. A *sura* is usually named by some catchword appearing in the text; thus the second is 'the Cow', because of a reference to a sacrifice of a cow which Moses demanded of the Israelites. None of this has much to do with content, and at this level the Koran is strikingly lacking in structure. A *sura* of any length will usually take up and dismiss a variety of topics in no obvious order, and a given topic may be treated in this way in several *sura*s. The largest effective units of structure thus tend to be blocks of verses which the formal organisation of the text does nothing to demarcate. Within such blocks, trivial dislocations are surprisingly frequent. God may appear in the first and third persons in one and the same sentence; there may be omissions which, if not made good by interpretation, render the sense unintelligible; there are even what look like grammatical errors. Whatever is behind these puzzling features, their preservation in our texts points to extraordinarily conservative editing, as if things had been kept just as they fell.

Yet alongside this conservative editing we also find evidence of a much freer handling of the raw materials of the Koran. This presumably reflects an earlier stage in their history. There are, for example, clear cases of interpolation. Thus in the fifty-third *sura*, the basic text consists of uniformly short verses in an inspired style, but in two places this is interrupted by a prosaic and prolix amplification which is stylistically quite out of place. Another significant feature is the frequency with which we find alternative versions of the same passage in different parts of the Koran; when placed side by side, these versions often show the same sort of variation as one finds between parallel versions of oral traditions. Whatever these phenomena mean, they presuppose very different processes from those at work in the final editing. It is also obvious that the Koran contains material in more than one style, and much effort has been expended on the elaboration of a relative chronology of the revelation on the assumption that short and inspired passages are likely to be older than long and prosaic ones.

Taken on its own, the Koran tells us very little about the events of Muhammad's career. It does not narrate these events, but merely refers to them; and in doing so, it has a tendency not to name names. Some do occur in contemporary contexts: four religious communities are named (Jews, Christians, Magians, and the mysterious Sabians), as are three Arabian deities (all female), three humans (of whom Muhammad is one), two ethnic groups (Quraysh and the Romans), and nine places. Of the places, four are mentioned in military connections (Badr, Mecca, Hunayn, Yathrib), and four are connected with the sanctuary (three of them we have already met in connection with the rites of pilgrimage, while the fourth is 'Bakka', said to be an alternative name for Mecca). The final place is Mount Sinai, which seems to be associated with the growing of olives. Leaving aside the ubiquitous Christians and Jews, none of these names occurs very often: Muhammad is named four or five times (once as 'Ahmad'), the Sabians thrice, Mount Sinai twice, and the rest once each. Identifying what the Koran is talking about in a contemporary context is therefore usually impossible without interpretation, which in previous chapters I have on occasion tacitly supplied. For such interpretation we are naturally dependent mainly on tradition. Without it we could probably infer that the protagonist of the Koran was Muhammad, that the scene of his life was in western Arabia, and that he bitterly resented the frequent dismissal of his claims to prophecy by his contemporaries. But we could not tell that the sanctuary was in Mecca, or that Muhammad himself came from there, and we could only guess that he established himself in Yathrib. We might indeed prefer a more northerly location altogether, on the grounds that the site of God's destruction of Lot's people (i.e. Sodom) is said to be one which those addressed pass by morning and night (K 37.137–8).

The Muslim scholars sought to relate the Koran to traditional information on Muhammad's life on two levels. First, they made a broad distinction between what was revealed in Mecca and what was revealed in Medina. Thus one early scholar is quoted for the rule of thumb according to which everything mentioning the 'communities' and 'generations' (i.e. of the past) is Meccan, and everything establishing legal obligations and norms is Medinese. This distinction has been broadly accepted by most modern scholars. Secondly, the Muslim scholars dealt in detail with the occasions on which particular passages were revealed. Thus Ibn Ishaq, treating the time when Muhammad had newly arrived in Medina, remarks that much of the revelation used to come down with reference to the Jewish rabbis, who kept asking him tricky questions. Ibn Ishaq then goes on to specify contexts for the revelation of numerous passages in these altercations between God and the Jews. In the face of many traditions of this kind, it is hard to dissent from the view of 'Abida al-Salmani, a scholar of the late seventh century, who is said to have refused to interpret a verse on the ground that those who had known the occasions of the revelation of the Koran had passed away. Most modern scholars discard the bulk of this material as without foundation, but retain some of the historically more significant links which it purports to establish between Koranic references and historical events.

The problem in such cases is how to distinguish between genuine historical information and material that came into existence to explain the very Koranic passages that concern us. An example will help to make this clear. In the third generation before Muhammad, as we saw in Chapter 2, Hashim and his brothers are said to have laid the foundations of Mecca's international trade. In the first place, tradition relates that Hashim initiated the two caravan journeys, that of the winter to the Yemen and that of the summer to Syria; these are known as the 'two *rihla*s', the word *rihla* simply meaning 'journey'. In the second place, he is reported to have led the way in a process whereby each brother went to negotiate with the ruler of one of the neighbouring states for the security of Meccan trade in their domains; at the same time, each brother on his way back made arrangements for the protection of commerce with the tribes along his route. These latter arrangements with the tribes went by the name of *ilaf*. There are naturally other versions of these traditions, sometimes differing considerably, but we can leave the variants aside.

Both these institutions are mentioned in the Koran. The first two verses of the 106th *sura* read: 'For the *ilaf* of Quraysh, their *ilaf* of the journey (*rihla*) of the winter and the summer.'

Koran and tradition thus appear to support each other's testimony in a most reassuring fashion, and confirm the historicity of these two foundations of Meccan trade. Yet by itself, the Koranic reference would not tell us much; *ilaf* is scarcely a term known outside this context, and a *rihla* could be any kind of journey. If we now turn to the commentators, we begin to have doubts. For one thing, it emerges that there was uncertainty as to how to read the word *ilaf* (the Arabic script being sparing in its marking of vowels) – which is surprising if the term was well-known. More important, there was a wide range of opinion among the commentators as to what the term meant, and it was not even agreed that the meaning had to do with commerce. It is as if future historians confronted by the term 'Common Market' in a twentieth-century document should speculate whether it meant a market catering to the needs of both sexes, or perhaps rather one frequented by the lower classes. Such a break in the continuity of the understanding of the Koran is not isolated. Many *sura*s, for example, begin with mysterious combinations of letters of the Arabic alphabet which must once have meant something to someone, but were already as opaque to the early Muslim scholars as they are to us.

It would seem, then, that as far as the commentators were concerned, God knew best what He meant by the term *ilaf*. Yet it is hard to believe that if *ilaf* was in fact a fundamental institution of Meccan trade, and was referred to as such in the Koran, the early commentators (many of them Meccans themselves) could have been so much at sea. The alternative hypothesis is that what we mistake for economic history is no more than the blossoming of one particular line of speculation to which an obscure Koranic verse has given rise. (Even the presumption that the 'journey of the winter and the summer' was commercial is uncertain; a distinguished authority who lived locally is quoted for the view that the reference is to a practice among Quraysh of spending the winter in Mecca and the summer in the nearby town of Ta'if.) Here too we have a phenomenon which may have far-reaching implications for Muhammad's biography.

External evidence

In this situation it would obviously be helpful to have some early sources that have not been transmitted within the Muslim tradition, or at least reflect only the earliest phase of it. A cave with some contemporary documents and diaries would meet the need admirably – but this is something we do not have, and probably never will. What we do have is nevertheless worthy of attention. It consists of two kinds of sources: Muslim material preserved archaeologically, and hence unaffected by the later development of tradition, and non-Muslim sources preserved in the literatures of non-Muslim communities. None of the material is earlier than the beginning of the conquest of the Fertile Crescent in 633–4, and much that is of interest is some decades later, but it can still take us behind the Muslim tradition in its eighth-century form. On the Muslim side, we can learn something from such sources as administrative papyri, coins and inscriptions, especially for the last years of the seventh century; the earliest datable papyrus fragments of religious content come only in the first half of the eighth century. On the non-Muslim side, we have a small body of material in Greek and Syriac dating from the time of the conquests, and further Syriac material from later in the century. An Armenian chronicler writing in the 660s gives us the earliest narrative account of Muhammad's career to survive in any language. In Hebrew, an eighth-century apocalypse has embedded in it an earlier apocalypse that seems to be contemporary with the conquests.

What does this material tell us? We may begin with the major points on which it agrees with the Islamic tradition. It precludes any doubts as to whether Muhammad was a real person: he is named in a Syriac source that is likely to date from the time of the conquests, and there is an account of him in a Greek source of the same period. From the 640s we have confirmation that the term *muhajir* was a central one in the new religion, since its followers are known as 'Magaritai' or 'Mahgraye' in Greek and Syriac respectively. At the same time, a papyrus of 643 is dated 'year twenty two', creating a strong presumption that something did happen in AD 622. The Armenian chronicler of the 660s attests that Muhammad was a merchant, and confirms the centrality of Abraham in his preaching. The Abrahamic sanctuary appears in an early Syriac source dated (insecurely) to the 670s.

Secondly, there are the major points on which this material is silent. It gives no indication that Muhammad's career unfolded in inner Arabia, and in particular makes no mention of Mecca; the Koran makes no appearance until the last years of the seventh century; and it is only then that we have any suggestion that the adherents of the new religion were called 'Muslims'. Since there is not much of this material anyway, such silences do not mean very much. We should nevertheless note that the earliest evidence from outside the tradition regarding the direction in which Muslims prayed, and by implication the location of their sanctuary, points much further north than Mecca. Equally, when the first Koranic quotations appear on coins and inscriptions towards the end of the seventh century, they show divergences from the canonical text. These are trivial from the point of view of content, but the fact that they appear in such formal contexts as these goes badly with the notion that the text had already been frozen.

Thirdly, there are the major disagreements. Two are

chronological. The first is that the Armenian chronicler's account of the foundation of Muhammad's community places it by implication several years after 622; here, however, the Islamic tradition has the support of the papyrus of 643. The second is that the earliest Greek source, which is dated to the year 634 and unlikely to be much later, speaks of Muhammad as still alive – two years after his death according to the Muslim tradition. There are indications that this impression was widely shared by the non-Muslim communities of the Fertile Crescent. The other two major disagreements are of considerable doctrinal interest, and relate to Muhammad's attitudes towards Palestine and the Jews.

To begin with the Jews, we have already seen how tradition preserves a document, the 'Constitution of Medina', in which Muhammad establishes a community to which believers and Jews alike belong, while retaining their different faiths. The document is anomalous and difficult, and could well be authentic in substance. Be that as it may, tradition goes on to recount a series of breaks between Muhammad and the Jews of Yathrib whereby the Jewish element was eliminated from the community several years before the conquests began. The early non-Muslim sources, by contrast, depict a relationship with the Jews at the time of the first conquests such as tradition concedes only for the first years of Muhammad's residence in Medina. The Armenian chronicler of the 660s describes Muhammad as establishing a community which comprised both Ishmaelites (i.e. Arabs) and Jews, with Abrahamic descent as their common platform; these allies then set off to conquer Palestine. The oldest Greek source makes the sensational statement that the prophet who had appeared among the Saracens (i.e. Arabs) was proclaiming the coming of the (Jewish) messiah, and speaks of 'the Jews who mix with the Saracens', and of the danger to life and limb of falling into the hands of these Jews and Saracens. We cannot easily dismiss this evidence as the product of Christian prejudice, since it finds confirmation in the Hebrew apocalypse referred to above. The break with the Jews is then placed by the Armenian chronicler immediately after the Arab conquest of Jerusalem.

The other major disagreement between the Muslim tradition and the non-Muslim sources is the place of Palestine in Muhammad's scheme of things. Palestine is far from unimportant in tradition (we saw how it tends to recover its centrality towards the end of time). Yet in the traditional account of Muhammad's career, it is already demoted in favour of Mecca in the second year of the *hijra*, when Muhammad changes the direction of prayer of his followers from Jerusalem to Mecca. Thereafter Mecca is the religious focus of his movement, as it is also the main object of his political and military aspirations. In the non-Muslim sources, by contrast, this role is played by Palestine, and provides the religious motive for its conquest. The Armenian chronicler further gives a rationale for this attachment: Muhammad told the Arabs that, as descendants of Abraham through Ishmael, they too had a claim to the land which God had promised to Abraham and his seed. The religion of Abraham is in fact as central in the Armenian account of Muhammad's preaching as it is in the Muslim sources; but it is given a quite different geographical twist.

If the external sources are in any significant degree right on such points, it would follow that tradition is seriously misleading on important aspects of the life of Muhammad, and that even the integrity of the Koran as his message is in some doubt. In view of what was said above about the nature of the Muslim sources, such a conclusion would seem to me legitimate; but it is only fair to add that it is not usually drawn.

8 Origins

To understand what Muhammad was doing in creating a new religion, it would be necessary to know what religious resources were available to him, and in what form. In a sense, of course, we know perfectly well; we possess rich literary remains from the Jewish and Christian traditions, and we know something about the paganism of Arabia. But beyond this point the going gets difficult. We might like to think of Muhammad as a well-travelled merchant acquainted with the same forms of the monotheist tradition as are familiar to us. Or we might think of him as a man of more local horizons who was in contact with some Arabian byways of monotheism which have otherwise left no trace. The first view makes him a man of considerable doctrinal originality, whereas on the second view he might have found much that to us is distinctively Islamic already present in his Arabian environment. The trouble is that we are not well-placed to decide between two such hypotheses. For example, we would dearly like to know what sort of Judaism was current in pre-Islamic western Arabia; but evidence of this is scarce within the Islamic tradition, and non-existent outside it. For the most part, we are reduced to the crude procedure of comparing Islam with the mainstream traditions of Judaism and Christianity, and trying to determine which elements came from which. The answers are often convincing, but they fail to tell us in what form these elements came to Muhammad, or he to them.

The Koran

One way of approaching the question is through the Koran,

which has been ransacked for parallels with the religious traditions of the day – not to mention others which may already have been extinct. The results of this research can perhaps be summarised as follows. First, nothing resembling the Koran as such is to be found in any other tradition; the book remains *sui generis*, and if it had predecessors, we know nothing of them. Secondly, there is no lack of elements in the Koran for which parallels can be found elsewhere, and these parallels are sometimes impressive. Thirdly, this evidence points in a bewildering variety of directions, and conforms to no simple pattern. The examples which follow should serve to bring this home.

As might be expected, Jewish influence is prominent. It can, for example, be seen in the way in which Biblical narratives are told in the Koran. Thus the story of the efforts of Potiphar's wife to seduce Joseph in Egypt appears in the Koran with the addition of a curious anecdote: the woman is irritated by the tittle-tattle of her peers, so she invites them to a banquet, gives each of them a knife, and orders Joseph to come before them; when he does so, they cut their hands (K 12.31). This story comes from post-Biblical Jewish tradition, and indeed it is only in the light of the Jewish original that the Koranic narrative becomes intelligible: the woman had set the gossips to cut up fruit with their knives, and they cut themselves inadvertently while staring at the good-looking Joseph.

We can take another example of Jewish influence from the vocabulary of religious law. The Koran enjoins the giving of alms, often conjoined with prayer as a basic duty of believers. The term for alms, *zakat*, is a loan-word in Arabic. In form it could be of either Jewish or Christian origin. But if we turn to the meaning, the field narrows. It is in Jewish texts from Palestine that we find the corresponding form used in the sense of the merit which accrues from good works; and in particular, we find a verbal form from the same root used in the sense of 'to give alms'. Christian usage, by contrast, offers no such parallel.

Other Koranic elements are definitely Christian in origin. Obvious examples are the material relating to the life of Jesus, and the legend of the Seven Sleepers of Ephesus (who appear in the Koran as 'the people of the cave'). Some of the religious loan-words found in the Koran are definitely or probably Christian; thus the term used for 'hypocrite' (*munafiq*) seems to be an Ethiopic Christian loan-word. These examples of Christian influence could easily be extended.

There is also the possibility of influences from other known monotheist groups. Thus the profession of faith that 'there is no god but God', and the emphasis on His having no companion, find their best (though not their only) parallel in Samaritanism, an archaic Jewish heresy which survived mainly in Palestine. But the real joker in the pack is the spectre of Judaeo-Christian influence. In the early Christian centuries there existed groups of Jewish Christians. Such groups combined an acceptance of the mission of Jesus with a retention of their Jewish observances; Jesus was for them no more than a man. We do not know what happened to these groups, but we do have an account which places a community of Jewish Christians in Jerusalem in the later seventh century. If such a group had influenced early Islam, this might account for much of the Koranic view of Jesus that we outlined above. On the other hand, it would not go well with the Koranic denial of the death of Jesus on the cross. This denial was a well-known Christian heresy (Docetism), and its primary appeal was to those who regarded Jesus as God, and were accordingly disturbed by the idea that God should have died. (Since the Koranic Jesus is so emphatically human, the appearance of this doctrine in the Koran is on any showing a puzzle.)

None of this excludes influences from outside the monotheist tradition. In particular, some Koranic prescriptions are more than likely to be endorsements of religious customs of pagan Arabia. A clear case is the practice of circumambulation which the Koran enjoins in connection with the rites of pilgrimage to the sanctuary. Muslim tradition presents this as a ritual that was current in pagan times, and a Christian source attests it (though not at a sanctuary) among the pre-Islamic Arabs of Sinai. Another case in point is the Arabian institution of a holy month or months, likewise associated with pilgrimage to a sanctuary, during which fighting is forbidden. As we saw, this custom is endorsed in the Koran, subject to the overriding demands of holy war. Here too, Muslim tradition describes the institution as one of pagan times, and the point is confirmed by a Greek account from the sixth century.

Key doctrines

It may be more interesting to approach the question of origins by picking out a couple of key elements of Muhammad's preaching and asking where they may have come from.

One quite fundamental idea is that of the 'religion of Abraham'. That this was not an invention of Muhammad's is indicated by the Islamic tradition: rightly or wrongly, it depicts adherents of the idea in both Mecca and Yathrib before the coming of Muhammad. Outside Arabia, we know that the idea had occurred, if only as armchair theology, to Jews and Christians. Long before Muhammad, the apocryphal Book of Jubilees (a Jewish work preserved by Christians) had outlined a religion of Abraham which the patriarch had imposed on all his sons and grandsons – including by implication the Arabs. The Jewish rabbis considered (and unsurprisingly rejected) the notion of an

Ishmaelite claim to Palestine by virtue of descent from Abraham. Sozomenus, a Christian writer of the fifth century, reconstructs a primitive Ishmaelite monotheism identical with that possessed by the Hebrews up to the time of Moses; and he goes on to argue from present conditions that Ishmael's laws must have been corrupted by the passage of time and the influence of pagan neighbours.

But did the Arabs themselves get to hear of these intriguing ideas? Here Sozomenus has something further to tell us. He remarks that (at a date later than his reconstructed history of the decay of the religion of Abraham) some Ishmaelite tribes happened to come in contact with Jews, and learnt from them about their 'true' origin, i.e. their descent from Ishmael; they then 'returned' to the observance of Hebrew laws and customs. Even at the present day, he adds, there are some Ishmaelites who live in the Jewish way. What Sozomenus is here describing is Arabs who adopted Jewish observances, not by becoming Jews, but by rediscovering their own Ishmaelite descent. All that is missing from this conception of the religion of Abraham is the Abrahamic sanctuary. This evidence is not lightly to be set aside: Sozomenus was a Palestinian from Gaza, and a casual remark indicates that he even knew something of Arabic poetry. We have no evidence that would show any direct link between this early religion of Abraham and Muhammad's message nearly two centuries later, but it is at least a confirmation that Muhammad was not the first in the field, and an indication of the use to which the Jewish brand of the monotheist tradition could be put by the Arabs.

Another fundamental feature of Muhammad's preaching is the set of political ideas which cluster around the notion of *hijra*. Although the Koran does not use *muhajir* in a Mosaic context, there are, as we saw, other points at which these ideas are linked to the story of Moses, and the overall analogy is striking. Likewise the Armenian chronicler makes a point of Muhammad's familiarity with the story of Moses. Yet in the seventh century this story was ancient history. The one context in which it was politically alive was Jewish messianism, a religious expectation which continued to fire occasional rebellions against a world dominated by gentiles. Here the career of the messiah was seen as a re-enactment of that of Moses; a key event in the drama was an exodus, or flight, from oppression into the desert, whence the messiah was to lead a holy war to reconquer Palestine. Given the early evidence connecting Muhammad with Jews and Jewish messianism at the time when the conquest of Palestine was initiated, it is natural to see in Jewish apocalyptic thought a point of departure for his political ideas.

In contrast to the diversity of origins that marks the Koranic material at large, both these points go well with the view that Muhammad owed more to Judaism than to Christianity. This would not be surprising. Both the Islamic tradition and – still more – the external sources portray him as having more to do with Jews than with Christians.

Conclusion

The Muslim profession of faith affirms that 'there is no god but God, and Muhammad is the messenger of God'. Only the first half of this affirmation conveys a substantive message; the second half merely identifies the bearer. In this sense, the burden of Muhammad's preaching was simply monotheism. Such an insistence was not superfluous in the seventh century. In Arabia, where an old-fashioned polytheism still flourished, it dramatically accelerated the penetration of the peninsula by monotheist influence. Outside Arabia, it had some purchase in the lands which the Arabs went on to conquer. Although authentic pagans were now in short supply, Zoroastrians and Christians were not immune to the challenge of a strict monotheism. The Zoroastrians worshipped not only the good god of their dualist cosmology, but sundry other deities as well; and while it may be true that the three persons of the Christian Trinity add up to one God without companions, the arithmetic is elusive, and not only to the theologically untrained. Only in the Jewish case does the monotheist polemic of Islam seem somewhat contrived. Muhammad, then, had a point. But this point was no more than the perennial message of monotheism, and as such it neither was, nor was intended to be, distinctive. It was what Muhammad made of this ancient verity that mattered; and in his day this meant what he made of it for the Arabs.

Muhammad and the Arabs

The reader may recollect that four Meccans are said to have experienced a revulsion from paganism in the generation before Muhammad, and that three of them ended up as Christians. The fourth, Zayd ibn 'Amr, is a more interesting figure. He set out from Mecca in quest of the religion of Abraham, and travelled to the Fertile Crescent. The choice was natural: where else could he hope to find such a treasury of religious expertise? Once there, he went about questioning monks and rabbis, but all to no purpose. Eventually he found a monk in the uplands to the east of Palestine who had something to tell him: there was no one at present who could guide him to the religion of Abraham, but a prophet was about to be sent to proclaim this religion – and would arise in the very land from which Zayd had set out. Zayd did not care for what he had seen of Judaism and Christianity, and he now set off on the long road back to Mecca. The Arab had wandered in vain; the truth was about to be revealed on his own doorstep.

With this we may compare the reactions of the Arabs and Jews of Yathrib to Muhammad's mission. As we saw, the first response came from the six men of Khazraj. They took Muhammad seriously because they had heard from their Jewish neighbours that a new prophet was about to appear. More precisely, tradition tells us that the Jews expected this prophet to lead them against the Arabs; so the Khazrajis were understandably anxious to appropriate Muhammad before the Jews could do so. Later we hear much of the hatred which the Jews felt for Muhammad. What they could not abide was that God had favoured the Arabs by choosing His messenger from among them. One Jew declared with a certain logic that he recognised Muhammad to be a true prophet, and would nevertheless oppose him as long as he lived.

These stories present two sides of the same coin. What was gall to the Jews was balm to the Arabs. The Jews, the original holders of the monotheist patent, now found themselves expropriated; the Arabs discovered that the truth they had humbly sought from the superior religious insight of monks and rabbis was in fact their own. Today such expropriations and discoveries take place under the banner of nationalism, but the motivation behind them is one which can come into play whenever men confront the problem of remaining themselves while adopting the beliefs of others.

What Muhammad also did for the Arabs of his day was to effect a powerful fusion between his monotheism and their tribal politics. His achievement can be seen as a revival of the radically monotheist polity enshrined in the story of Moses. By the time of Muhammad, the Jews had for long lived the life of a dispossessed minority; their messianic attempts to restore their political fortunes were sporadic and short-lived. Christianity had fared differently. It had put itself out to assure the Roman authorities that it was not a subversive religion, and in due course these authorities had come to see it as one which might do the state some service. Thereafter the Roman Empire was Christianised, much to the disgust of its pagan aristocracy; but it was in no sense a monotheist creation. Against such a background, it was a very considerable innovation to bring about the rule of God and His prophet over an independent community of believers.

It was no accident that Muhammad achieved this in Arabia, with its predominantly pastoral and stateless tribal society. He had the good luck to be born into an environment which offered scope for political creativity such as is not usually open to the religious reformer. But it was clearly more than good luck that he found in this society the key to a hitherto virtually untapped reserve of power. The pastoral tribes of Arabia were of necessity mobile and warlike, but their military potential was normally dissipated in small-scale raiding and feuding. Muhammad's doctrine, and the use he put it to, brought to this society a remarkable, if transient, coherence of

purpose. Without it, it is hard to see how the Arabian tribesmen could have gone on to conquer so substantial a portion of
the known world.

The Arab conquests rapidly destroyed one empire, and
permanently detached large territories of another. This was,
for the states in question, an appalling catastrophe, but it need
not have marked the end of the road. Political unity did not
come easily to the Arab tribesmen, and within decades of
Muhammad's death they had fought two major civil wars. It
was not unreasonable to suppose that the Arab domination
would simply disintegrate, leaving as little residue as did that
of the Goths in Europe. In any case, tribal conquerors are
usually less civilised than the settled populations they subject,
and accordingly end up by adopting the culture of their sub-
jects. Of this too there were signs in the early period of Arab
rule. Had the Arabs either disintegrated politically or capitu-
lated culturally in this formative period, the minor religious
movement initiated by Muhammad in western Arabia would
not have become one of the world's major civilisations. That
the Arabs were able to withstand the countervailing pressures
so successfully in the generations following the death of their
prophet is remarkable. It is hard to imagine that they could
have done so had their hegemony not derived meaning and
purpose from the monotheist polity which Muhammad had
created among them, and the monotheist faith which he had
made their own.

Something of this meaning and purpose can perhaps be
conveyed by a numismatic comparison. Jesus, who like
Muhammad was often asked awkward questions, was once
challenged by the Pharisees to say whether it was lawful 'to
give tribute unto Caesar'. Jesus had them show him a coin,
and asked in return: 'Whose is this image and superscription?'
When they answered that it was Caesar's, Jesus gave his

famous reply: 'Render therefore unto Caesar the things which are Caesar's; and unto God the things that are God's' (Matt. 22.15–22). It was an apt and prudent distinction, a dignified solution to the problem of confuting the Pharisees without giving offence to the local representatives of imperial Rome. Over six hundred years later, and some sixty years after the death of Muhammad, the Caliph 'Abd al-Malik – who did as much as anyone for the political unity and cultural autonomy of the Arabs – likewise gave his attention to the matter of coins, their images and superscriptions. A silver coin struck in the year 79 (AD 698–9) is a good example of the results of his deliberations. There is no image, but there is an abundance of more or less Koranic superscription. On the obverse is the legend: 'There is no god but God, alone, without companion'; and on the reverse: 'Muhammad is the messenger of God, whom He sent with guidance and the religion of truth, to make it supreme above all others, whether the polytheists like it or not.'

Muhammad and the wider world

As we saw, there are already indications in the Koran that Muhammad's message was in principle directed to all mankind. One of his immediate followers was in fact a Persian, a certain Salman, who had abandoned the religion of his fathers, left his native land, and come to Arabia in search of the religion of Abraham. Within a century or two of Muhammad's death, the religion of Abraham was spread far beyond Arabia, and large numbers of converts to Islam had appeared among the conquered peoples. At first conversion tended to go hand in hand with Arabisation – in other words, the converts were assimilated into the society of their conquerors. But in both social and geographical terms, Islam soon spread well beyond the reach of such Arabisation.

Today, the Arabian prophet is recognised as the messenger of God among a great variety of peoples, and the Arabs themselves account for less than a sixth of the world's Muslims. It is of course true that Muhammad's religion, with its Arabian sanctuary and Arabic Koran, retains a strong Arab colouring; unlike Christianity, it did not break with the milieu in which it was born. Yet the Arab identity of Islam has inevitably faded with the centuries, and Islam is now many things to many men.

There is no place in this book for an analysis of the way in which Muhammad's legacy was developed, extended, attenuated and transformed among generations born at times and places increasingly removed from his own. Even the Caliph 'Abd al-Malik had never met Muhammad; since his day over forty generations of Muslims have lived and died, and the history they have made can hardly be laid at the door of a man who claimed neither to possess the treasures of God nor to know the future, and followed only what was revealed to him.

Nor is there any place here for a consideration of the absolute value of Muhammad's message. He saw himself, according to the tradition, as the last brick in the edifice of monotheist prophecy. Today we live in a landscape littered with the fallen masonry of such edifices; what are we, for whom bricks are but clay, to see in Muhammad's contribution to this scene? Any answer to such a question is bound to be intensely arbitrary, and I shall therefore seek only to identify that quality of Islam which has most worked on me in the writing of this book. Both Judaism and Christianity are religions of profound pathos – Judaism with its dream of ethnic redemption from present wretchedness, Christianity with its individual salvation through the sufferings of a God of love. In each case the pathos is indeed moving; but it is a pathos which too easily appeals to the emotion of self-pity. Islam, in contrast, is strikingly free of this temptation. The bleakness which we saw in its conception of the relationship between God and man is the authentic, unadulterated bleakness of the universe itself.

Further reading

Two of the primary sources on which this book is based are readily available in English.

There are many translations of the Koran. I have made most use of that by A. J. Arberry (*The Koran interpreted*, first published in two volumes, London and New York, 1955, but more easily accessible in the Oxford University Press series 'The World's Classics', London, 1964). Contrary to what the title might suggest, it gives a bare (but palatable) translation, which delicately conveys the obscurities of the original without resolving them. An old translation which has worn very well is that of George Sale (*The Koran*, London, 1734, many times reprinted). The great virtue of Sale's translation is that it presents the text in a context of traditional Sunni interpretation, while making it clear by the use of italics and footnotes what is, and is not, contained in the text itself. The standard European translation today is a German one by R. Paret. My references to the Koran are by *sura* and verse: 'K 2.10' means the tenth verse of the second *sura*. There is more than one way of numbering Koranic verses; I follow that of G. Flügel's edition of the Koran, since it is used by Arberry.

The *Sira* of Ibn Ishaq as transmitted by Ibn Hisham has been translated into English by A. Guillaume (*The life of Muhammad*, London, 1955), and my references (as: 'S 154') are to the pages of his translation. It is, however, too bulky a book for all but the most intrepid beginner; an annotated translation of Ma'mar ibn Rashid's account as transmitted by 'Abd al-Razzaq ibn Hammam would be a welcome addition to the literature.

Turning to modern writing, there is no lack of introductory works. Thus for the life of Muhammad, there are readable accounts by W. M. Watt (*Muhammad: prophet and statesman*, London, 1961, itself an epitome of two larger volumes by the same author) and by M. Rodinson (*Mohammed*, London, 1971). A shorter account that carries the story through to the conquests is F. Gabrieli, *Muhammad and the conquests of Islam*, London, 1968. For the Koran, a useful introduction is *Bell's Introduction to the Qur'ān*, revised by W. M. Watt (Edinburgh, 1970). For a survey of Islam which relates Muhammad to the subsequent evolution of the religion, see I. Goldziher, *Introduction to Islamic theology and law*, Princeton, N. J., 1981 (a translation of an old but excellent German work which also covers Sufism and sectarian divisions, both of them topics excluded from the scope of this book).

There is a large volume of modern research on the topics covered in this book, but a surprising lack of up-to-date standard works. There is no such thing as a critical edition of the Koran. There used to be a standard work on the Koran in German (T. Nöldeke and others, *Geschichte des Qorāns*, second edition, Leipzig, 1909–38), and it remains indispensable for serious study; but with the steady appearance of new material (which may well continue into the coming century), the work in question is becoming obsolete in many particulars. Much the same is true for Muhammad's life, where again the standard work was in German (F. Buhl, *Das Leben Muhammeds*, Leipzig, 1930, originally published in Danish). The reader who wishes to go beyond the few English works mentioned in this note will, however, find much information and current bibliography in relevant articles of the second edition of *The Encyclopaedia of Islam*, Leiden and London, 1960– (e.g. the articles 'Ḳur'ān' and 'Muhammad').

A few references may be added for the more recondite information used here and there in this book. For the external sources discussed in the last section of Chapter 7, references will be found in Chapter 1 of Patricia Crone and Michael Cook, *Hagarism: the making of the Islamic world*, Cambridge, 1977. For Sozomenus' account of the religion of Abraham (above, p. 81), see his *Ecclesiastical History*, VI, 38; I owe my knowledge of this passage to Patricia Crone. For the Jewish usage of the verb *zakki* in the sense of 'to give alms' (above, pp. 78–9), see for example *Leviticus Rabbah*, 34.5–14 (in the new edition of M. Margulies, Jerusalem 1953–60); this testimony seems to have been overlooked by Islamicists.

Index

OXFORD

MORE OXFORD PAPERBACKS

This book is just one of nearly 1000 Oxford Paperbacks currently in print. If you would like details of other Oxford Paperbacks, including titles in the World's Classics, Oxford Reference, Oxford Books, OPUS, Past Masters, Oxford Authors, and Oxford Shakespeare series, please write to:

UK and Europe: Oxford Paperbacks Publicity Manager, Arts and Reference Publicity Department, Oxford University Press, Walton Street, Oxford OX2 6DP.

Customers in UK and Europe will find Oxford Paperbacks available in all good bookshops. But in case of difficulty please send orders to the Cash-with-Order Department, Oxford University Press Distribution Services, Saxon Way West, Corby, Northants NN18 9ES. Tel: 01536 741519; Fax: 01536 746337. Please send a cheque for the total cost of the books, plus £1.75 postage and packing for orders under £20; £2.75 for orders over £20. Customers outside the UK should add 10% of the cost of the books for postage and packing.

USA: Oxford Paperbacks Marketing Manager, Oxford University Press, Inc., 200 Madison Avenue, New York, N.Y. 10016.

Canada: Trade Department, Oxford University Press, 70 Wynford Drive, Don Mills, Ontario M3C 1J9.

Australia: Trade Marketing Manager, Oxford University Press, G.P.O. Box 2784Y, Melbourne 3001, Victoria.

South Africa: Oxford University Press, P.O. Box 1141, Cape Town 8000.

MASTERS

PAST MASTERS

A wide range of unique, short, clear introductions to the lives and work of the world's most influential thinkers. Written by experts, they cover the history of ideas from Aristotle to Wittgenstein. Readers need no previous knowledge of the subject, so they are ideal for students and general readers alike.

Each book takes as its main focus the thought and work of its subject. There is a short section on the life and a final chapter on the legacy and influence of the thinker. A section of further reading helps in further research.

The series continues to grow, and future Past Masters will include **Owen Gingerich** on *Copernicus*, **R G Frey** on *Joseph Butler*, **Bhiku Parekh** on *Gandhi*, **Christopher Taylor** on *Socrates*, **Michael Inwood** on *Heidegger*, and **Peter Ghosh** on *Weber*.

MASTERS

KEYNES

Robert Skidelsky

John Maynard Keynes is a central thinker of the twentieth century. This is the only available short introduction to his life and work.

Keynes's doctrines continue to inspire strong feelings in admirers and detractors alike. This short, engaging study of his life and thought explores the many positive and negative stereotypes and also examines the quality of Keynes's mind, his cultural and social milieu, his ethical and practical philosophy, and his monetary thought. Recent scholarship has significantly altered the treatment and assessment of Keynes's contribution to twentieth-century economic thinking, and the current state of the debate initiated by the Keynesian revolution is discussed in a final chapter on its legacy.

MASTERS

RUSSELL

A. C. Grayling

Bertrand Russell (1872–1970) is one of the most famous and important philosophers of the twentieth century. In this account of his life and work A. C. Grayling introduces both his technical contributions to logic and philosophy, and his wide-ranging views on education, politics, war, and sexual morality. Russell is credited with being one of the prime movers of Analytic Philosophy, and with having played a part in the revolution in social attitudes witnessed throughout the twentieth-century world. This introduction gives a clear survey of Russell's achievements across their whole range.

OXFORD PAPERBACK REFERENCE

From *Art and Artists* to *Zoology*, the Oxford Paperback Reference series offers the very best subject reference books at the most affordable prices.

Authoritative, accessible, and up to date, the series features dictionaries in key student areas, as well as a range of fascinating books for a general readership. Included are such well-established titles as Fowler's *Modern English Usage*, Margaret Drabble's *Concise Companion to English Literature*, and the bestselling science and medical dictionaries.

The series has now been relaunched in handsome new covers. Highlights include new editions of some of the most popular titles, as well as brand new paperback reference books on *Politics*, *Philosophy*, and *Twentieth-Century Poetry*.

With new titles being constantly added, and existing titles regularly updated, Oxford Paperback Reference is unrivalled in its breadth of coverage and expansive publishing programme. New dictionaries of *Film*, *Economics*, *Linguistics*, *Architecture*, *Archaeology*, *Astronomy*, and *The Bible* are just a few of those coming in the future.

Oxford
Paperback
Reference

THE OXFORD DICTIONARY OF PHILOSOPHY

Edited by Simon Blackburn

* 2,500 entries covering the entire span of the subject including the most recent terms and concepts

* Biographical entries for nearly 500 philosophers

* Chronology of philosophical events

From Aristotle to Zen, this is the most comprehensive, authoritative, and up to date dictionary of philosophy available. Ideal for students or a general readership, it provides lively and accessible coverage of not only the Western philosophical tradition but also important themes from Chinese, Indian, Islamic, and Jewish philosophy. The paperback includes a new Chronology.

'an excellent source book and can be strongly recommended . . . there are generous and informative entries on the great philosophers . . . Overall the entries are written in an informed and judicious manner.'
Times Higher Education Supplement

Oxford
Paperback
Reference

THE CONCISE OXFORD DICTIONARY
OF POLITICS

Edited by Iain McLean

Written by an expert team of political scientists from Warwick University, this is the most authoritative and up-to-date dictionary of politics available.

* Over 1,500 entries provide truly international coverage of major political institutions, thinkers and concepts

* From Western to Chinese and Muslim political thought

* Covers new and thriving branches of the subject, including international political economy, voting theory, and feminism

* Appendix of political leaders

* Clear, no-nonsense definitions of terms such as veto and subsidiarity

Oxford
Paperback
Reference

THE CONCISE OXFORD COMPANION TO ENGLISH LITERATURE

Edited by Margaret Drabble and Jenny Stringer

Derived from the acclaimed *Oxford Companion to English Literature*, the concise maintains the wide coverage of its parent volume. It is an indispensable, compact guide to all aspects of English literature. For this revised edition, existing entries have been fully updated and revised with 60 new entries added on contemporary writers.

* **Over 5,000 entries on the lives and works of authors, poets and playwrights**

* **The most comprehensive and authoritative paperback guide to English literature**

* **New entries include Peter Ackroyd, Martin Amis, Toni Morrison, and Jeanette Winterson**

* **New appendices list major literary prize-winners**

From the reviews of its parent volume:

'It earns its place at the head of the best sellers: every home should have one'
Sunday Times

RETHINKING LIFE AND DEATH
THE COLLAPSE OF OUR TRADITIONAL ETHICS

Peter Singer

A victim of the Hillsborough Disaster in 1989, Anthony Bland lay in hospital in a coma being fed liquid food by a pump, via a tube passing through his nose and into his stomach. On 4 February 1993 Britain's highest court ruled that doctors attending him could lawfully act to end his life.

Our traditional ways of thinking about life and death are collapsing. In a world of respirators and embryos stored for years in liquid nitrogen, we can no longer take the sanctity of human life as the cornerstone of our ethical outlook.

In this controversial book Peter Singer argues that we cannot deal with the crucial issues of death, abortion, euthanasia and the rights of nonhuman animals unless we sweep away the old ethic and build something new in its place.

Singer outlines a new set of commandments, based on compassion and commonsense, for the decisions everyone must make about life and death.

OXFORD

FOUR ESSAYS ON LIBERTY

Isaiah Berlin

'those who value liberty for its own sake believe that to be free to choose, and not to be chosen for, is an inalienable ingredient in what makes human beings human'
Introduction to *Four Essays On Liberty*

Political Ideas in the Twentieth Century
Historical Inevitability
Two Concepts of Liberty
John Stuart Mill and the Ends of Life

These four essays deal with the various aspects of individual liberty, including the distinction between positive and negative liberty and the necessity of rejecting determinism if we wish to keep hold of the notions of human responsibility and freedom.

'practically every paragraph introduces us to half a dozen new ideas and as many thinkers—the landscape flashes past, peopled with familiar and unfamiliar people, all arguing incessantly'
New Society